how to start a home-based

Handyman Business

Terry Meany

Guilford, Connecticut

Copyright © 2009 by Morris Book Publishing, LLC

Text design: Sheryl P. Kober
Layout Artist: Kim Burdick

Library of Congress Cataloging-in-Publication Data
Meany, Terry.
 How to start a home-based handyman business / Terry Meany.
     p. cm.
 Includes index.
 ISBN 978-0-7627-5277-5
1. Dwellings—Maintenance and repair. 2. Repairing trades—Management. 3. Home-based businesses—Management. I. Title.
 TH4815.M43 2009
 690'.24—dc22

                                    2009018281

Printed in the United States of America

10 9 8 7 6 5 4 3 2 1

Contents

Introduction

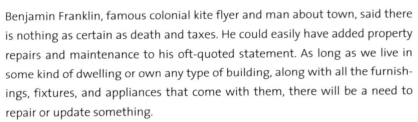

Benjamin Franklin, famous colonial kite flyer and man about town, said there is nothing as certain as death and taxes. He could easily have added property repairs and maintenance to his oft-quoted statement. As long as we live in some kind of dwelling or own any type of building, along with all the furnishings, fixtures, and appliances that come with them, there will be a need to repair or update something.

The wear and tear of daily life takes a toll on floors, paint and drywall, kitchen faucets—just about everything we touch and use. Throw kids and dogs into the mix, and there will always be nicks, gouges, broken windows, and sticking doors to fix.

The question is: Who's going to do those repairs? There's a good chance it will be you.

Homeowners come in all shapes and sizes, and with them come differing degrees of Mr. and Ms. Fix-It abilities. A few will try anything; others can't tell a hammer from a can opener; and a fair number will attempt small jobs and happily farm out the others. It's a matter of skill as well as economics. If someone isn't especially skilled in plumbing, for instance, and losing the use of a bathroom while learning how to repair a toilet really isn't an option, then it's time to call in some help.

The more money someone earns, the less economical it is to tie up time cleaning gutters or replacing light switches. It's going to be more cost-effective to hire someone with expertise, knowing the job will be done correctly and in good time. Sure, there's great satisfaction in doing repairs yourself and solving problems, but frustration often trumps gratification when the roof is leaking and overnight guests are coming.

That's where you, the handyman, come in. You will be the one who buys a home-owner time, resolves dilemmas, provides relief, and assures that life will go on, intact. If you did a good job the first time, you'll be called back for the next breakdown. You probably won't get invited to any of the kids' weddings (then again, you might), but you'll be high up on the speed dial.

Once upon a time, or so the story goes, Dad or Grandpa or Uncle Bill could fix just about anything. Mom or Grandma or Aunt Betty could fix things, too, but the story usually mentions just the boys. The story also conveniently forgets the painters, plumbers, roofers, and electricians that were regularly hired when the family handyman was flummoxed. There will always be a need—a well-paid need—for a competent handyman. It seems that with every passing era, the basic repair skills that once were passed down by intent or observation from one generation to another are passed on less and less. If passed on at all.

(And although the less-than-definitive term *handyperson* avoids what could be deemed the sexist job title of *handyman*, or the awkward *handyman/handywoman*, I'll stick with the easier, traditional title. Of course, every reader can entertain any desired name for a new handyman business, including Jill of Many Trades [Master of Some], Buster's Bust-It Repair Service, or Get Your Fix.)

Let's face it—with more of us working longer hours and commuting longer distances to our jobs, one of the last things a homeowner wants to do on days off is muck around the house doing nuisance repairs. Even in times of economic hardship, repairs must be made. The handyman business is a product of our times, so much so that handyman franchises exist from coast to coast. Buying a franchise is one approach to get into the business, but you've purchased this book to run your own show and to wear all the hats—director, lead actor, stagehand, and chief of payroll—not the company uniform of a national corporation.

One advantage of the handyman business is the low entry cost. You don't need thousands of dollars in plumbing tools, a large truck, or crews of employees. Sometimes you only need a small toolbox, as did one handyman I heard of in Seattle who specialized in rewiring and installing doorbells. Window washing is another handyman service that requires almost no tools other than a bucket, some sponges, squee-gees, cleaner, rags, and a ladder. You can start small, perhaps filling a niche such as pressure-washing, and then work your way into a broader scope of work. You can even keep your day job while you expand your handyman business. You'll know when you're ready to jump in full-time.

Starting a business and becoming self-employed can be intimidating. You'll have no one to fall back on but yourself, no salary except what you can generate day after day, and no perks other than what you can provide. There will be days when you wonder why you left the security (really, the illusion of security) of an established job with a steady paycheck and benefits.

Then you'll remind yourself that you have no supervisor to answer to and no workplace policies you disagree with (but have to abide by anyway). To some extent, you can pick your own hours (and will most likely work more of them than you would like to at first). And there's no end to the satisfaction of confronting a new problem, figuring out a solution, and walking away with the thanks of your customers. Humans are built to solve problems, yet some people never get the opportunity to solve much of anything in their jobs. Problem solving keeps you sharp and challenges your mind. It challenges your body, too, when you have to figure out how to remove an oversized door by yourself without damaging anything, or install hardware you're unfamiliar with.

And you *will* figure it out; it comes with the territory of running your own business.

Working alone isn't for everyone—although you will meet new people every week, from suppliers to customers to other contractors. This in itself can invigorate and lead to surprising relationships and opportunities. I've met a number of small contractors over the years who gradually invested in real estate they learned about from their clients, buying direct before the properties went on the market. Others, in the course of their jobs, haul out and remove (for a fee) perfectly usable goods, from dishwashers to furniture, that are no longer wanted by their owners. Many of these goods become salable items or are used by handymen themselves. One hauler I met in San Francisco had a garage full of such items he was saving for a large and no doubt profitable yard sale. Another had a sale every year from his collected goods.

Along the way, you'll learn more tricks of the trade, have some of the most frustrating days imaginable, and some of the best. Customers will run the gamut of human personalities: from generous to cheap, from grateful to suspicious, or even uninterested. The vast majority will be positive, and will appreciate a job well done. Go beyond their expectations and you will gain a long-term client and a great source of referrals. Do a poor job, or let a problem go unresolved, and that same customer will be referring to you for all the wrong reasons.

There is plenty of handyman business to go around. As in any business, the better you perform and the more superior customer service you offer, the better your chances of success. These are not difficult principles. The simple courtesies of returning phone calls promptly, showing up on time, and maintaining a neat job site will be long remembered—and profitable.

Remember—everyone can use a handyman, and that handyman could be you.

01 So You Want to Start a Home-Based Handyman Business

Congratulations—Or Should You Run for the Hills?

According to the Small Business Administration's Office of Advocacy, there were 27.2 million small businesses in the United States in 2007 (the SBA defines a small business as an independent business with fewer than 500 employees). Over 20 million of these businesses had no employees, meaning only their owners, or sole proprietors, were working. Over 637,000 new small businesses opened in 2007 alone.

Think of it: Almost 9 percent of the population has gone into business for themselves, from dry cleaners to therapists to handymen such as you, all deciding to put up a sign and announce to the world they are open for work. These individuals have chosen self-reliance, trust in their abilities, a certain faith in the marketplace, and a hopeful roll of the dice over working for someone else and the presumed safety of a paycheck and benefits.

Are they all crazy?

When another statistic is considered—the over half a million small businesses that close every year—you have to wonder. Why not stay at a sure thing, a job that direct-deposits money into your checking account a couple of times a month, provides two weeks of paid vacation, and throws in some kind of medical coverage?

Because there is no sure thing, as any economic downturn, corporate change of fortune, or company buyout teaches us. Few people stay in the same job or career for a lifetime any longer, waiting for a pension to pay out—if it does pay out. Multiple careers and job changes are now the norm. Entire industries fade before our eyes . . . but this is nothing new (seen any blacksmiths lately?). Being left to your own devices and joining those who work for themselves can be very appealing compared with a less-than-reliable job market.

The Eternal Handyman

Computer programmers will come and go. Travel agents will continually get replaced by online travel sites. Even radiologists are outsourced overseas. But the Internet can't repair a broken window or patch a hole in a roof. There will always be a need for someone, a handyman, to arrive on-site and fix things. Until this work becomes mechanized (and performed by traveling robots), you will always be able to find work, and plenty of willing customers.

Knowing how to do repairs is only one part of starting your business. How you run the business will determine your financial success and viability.

Keep in mind that the handyman business is multifaceted. You're not just fixing things; you're providing a service as well as selling products (locksets, faucets, paint). You offer knowledgeable information and solutions to specific repair problems. A handyman must:

- schedule and manage a daily and weekly workload;
- pick up materials;
- write up billings;
- hire and train any employees; and
- stay educated about new materials and repair techniques.

Turning Skills and Work Experience into a Business

The entertainment industry has a very skewed view of doctors. In movies and television shows, plastic surgeons and neurosurgeons transform themselves into family practitioners, *just like that!* In real life, this doesn't happen for a lot of reasons, among them the fact that being a family doctor or general practitioner requires a very different base of knowledge than that used by a surgeon drilling into a skull or reshaping a nose. Just because you can repair a faucet or hang a door doesn't mean you have the skills to run a business repairing faucets and hanging doors. You need different skills.

What will you need to know? How about:

- Basic accounting
- Estimating and bidding
- Time management
- Money management

- Customer relations
- Employee relations (if you have employees)
- All legal issues related to running your business
- How to deal with a job gone bad
- When to say no

Some of these skills simply come with time and experience. Practice will never make perfect—there's no such thing as perfection—but you will improve. Reading this book as well as hearing the stories of other small business owners can save you some mishaps, but in the same way you fell off your bike a few times before mastering it, you won't completely escape them.

What's the biggest requirement? It's the motivation that drives every business owner: the desire to work for yourself.

Part-Time Handyman

Opening a handyman business doesn't have to be a full-time pursuit—not at first, or not ever. Plenty of successful small businesses exist alongside their owners' day jobs. Keep in mind that frequent weekend and evening work brings with it a personal toll (all work and no play . . .). If you see your handyman business as supplemental (as opposed to critical) to your normal income, you can adjust your hours accordingly. If you're transitioning out of a job or career, you have the option of waiting until you have a comfortable customer and referral base before going full-time. Even as a side business, you'll still have to follow all state and federal tax, licensing, and insurance requirements.

Self-Employment: Being Your Own Boss—Or Is Everyone Your Boss?

Working for someone else means you show up and perform. The infrastructure is present, the lights are working, you have a desk or truck to work from, and payroll gives you a pay stub every two weeks after conveniently taking taxes out. If you're smarter than your boss or have better ideas, but you go unrecognized, that's life. Many people willingly live this life, and that's a good thing, because if everyone went around working for themselves, we would still be living in huts and trading from one person to the next. Our modern way of life couldn't exist without large businesses and governments with lots of employees.

For those who simply must supervise themselves and thrive on the risks and rewards, self-employment is the only way to go. You will never be happy or fulfilled without at least trying it. Like any other path in life, it has advantages and disadvantages.

Advantages

- Greater sense of freedom
- Potential for higher income
- Shorter commute
- Living by your decisions
- Easier to schedule free time
- Opportunities to learn new skills
- Meeting new people

Disadvantages

- Requires more self-discipline
- Income can decrease
- Longer commute is possible
- Higher FICA taxes
- Demanding customers
- Taking on less-than-preferred jobs for the income
- Loneliness—you no longer have regular colleagues

Most of the self-employed contractors I know couldn't stand working for anyone else. They had to strike out on their own, and for the most part, they make comfortable, successful livings. They could not survive in a corporate setting, whether working on a production line or in a manager's office. They have to run their own shows. Does this sound like you? Then it's time to plan your "entrance strategy" into the handyman business.

Franchise Opportunities

Like the fast-food industry, there are franchise opportunities available nationwide in the handyman business, as an Internet search will readily show. This is one route into the industry, but more in a managerial role (one franchisor cheerfully states they don't expect you to do any of the handyman work, only run the franchise). Bear in mind that you will be following company rules and paying fees for doing so. The trade-off is whatever status and financial gain a corporate franchise might bring you. Carefully research a prospective franchisor and be sure you fully understand the terms and conditions of signing on.

What Can You Offer That's Unique or Different?

As a handyman, you can offer specialized services that set you apart from your competitors. I had a business repairing old wood windows, and for years, I nearly had a monopoly on it in the Seattle area. Other contractors would do similar repairs from time to time, but not as a full-time business. The work wasn't especially complicated, but I had plenty of customers.

Can you do spot refinishing on damaged furniture or floors, blending in the new finish so well that no one can tell a repair was needed? How about invisible repairs to drywall tape, or cracks in concrete? Are you a whiz at building and installing shelving? Digging drainage ditches for wet yards full of landscaping and lawns? These are all tasks that property owners need done, but don't want to call in a specialty contractor to do them.

Are you more of a generalist, without any specific trade skill that stands out as exceptional? Sometimes all it takes is a memorable personality or demeanor to set you apart—more *how* you do something than what you do. Word of mouth spreads very fast on Web sites, and from person to person as well. A favorable impression goes a long way toward keeping old customers and finding new ones.

Integrity on the Job

Sometimes, telling a potential customer they *shouldn't* go ahead with a job is a way to stand out. Some repairs simply won't last, and replacement is a better choice. Convincing a customer of this, even if it means someone else will do the work—say, a gutter contractor replacing a damaged gutter system rather than you trying to patch it up—shows your integrity. There's a good chance you'll be remembered the next time a repair is needed.

Show Me the Money

Satisfaction from your labors and self-determination in your work—in this case, running your own handyman business—are wonderful goals. However, they're hard to accomplish if the money isn't there. Money might not buy happiness, but not having it doesn't help matters much, either. You need to address some financial basics, and address them realistically, if you're going to choose self-employment (this will be discussed in more detail in chapters 3 and 4).

Regardless of whose data you read, Americans come up short in the personal savings category. In recent years, *negative* savings rates have even been recorded. If you're in this category of citizens, and do not want to borrow money to tide you over as you start your handyman business, think twice about timing your start. Putting off your dream for a year or so is preferable to having it become an underfinanced nightmare.

Standard financial advice calls for six months' living expenses tucked aside for emergencies—an emergency meaning you're out of a job and have no income. The six-month figure might have been plucked from someone's horoscope for all its scientific validity, but it's a good figure to stick with. Six months gives you a comfortable financial cushion—but is it enough? Like so much else, it depends.

The B Word—Budget

You'll need to figure out what you're spending, and this means making a budget. There are plenty of personal budget forms available online, and they don't require Excel programs to create them. Your budget will list your expenses, including:

- Rent or mortgage
- Average utility bills
- Insurance
- Automobile and transportation expenses
- Home maintenance costs
- Food
- Credit card payments
- Child-related expenses
- Anything else

Once you know what you're spending, you'll know how much you need to save for your emergency fund. You'll also know how much you'll need to earn to maintain your lifestyle.

Reality is important here when it comes to listing what you're spending, how much you expect to earn, and how fast you can collect on it. Given that most handyman jobs require less than a day's work and that payment is expected upon completion, you should collect quite quickly. In a sense, your business follows a retail model: Payment is due when services have been rendered.

Be as conservative as possible in your projected earnings, and avoid new debt. Plenty of businesses close because they're unable to pay their expenses. Fortunately, the handyman business has modest start-up costs, so many of your money issues will focus on dealing with the loss of a previously steady paycheck as you replace it with income from your new venture.

Be Realistic about Earnings

If you're married or living with a partner who works, and you both have a clear understanding of your handyman business, then you'll have an income you can fall back on as your business grows. You should both be in agreement about time frames, too—meaning, who's paying for what, and for how long. Otherwise, it can become not surprisingly muddied and unpleasant.

Once you've mulled over the money issues—and we're only just beginning here—you have to address the other big one: you. Are you prepared for self-employment and the roles of a small business owner?

Personality Profile

Do you know what kind of personality you have? Your friends or family have surely told you you're serious, funny, outgoing, quiet, or any number of other observations. Different schools of psychology have more definitive personality types based on how sociable you are, whether you're a doer, judger, feeler, and how much of each quality you possess, based on tests and personal inventories.

Guess what? It doesn't make much difference. If you're introverted, you'll become more extroverted and cheery when it comes time to wooing customers. Are you already extroverted? Do you like to gab (constantly)? Tone it down or you'll never get any work done, and you'll drive your customers crazy. I've known several independent contractors like this. They start their days a bit on the late side, have coffee with their clients, talk for an hour or so, work for an hour or so, then, more coffee and talk. One did about three hours' worth of work a day; another always required more time to finish jobs than he estimated; and the third drove his clients slowly but surely insane.

No good with math? Too bad; you'll have to face it and improve, or your numbers will never work out, and you'll lose money and waste time. You'll find yourself underestimating the materials required to do a job and then making unnecessary trips to a supplier; these trips do not pay for themselves. If you're slow getting your paperwork done, you'll be slow in getting paid. You can't avoid numbers and math when you run your own business.

Estimating Accurately

Establishing unit costs for your work—so much to install so many feet of baseboard, or strip and wax so many square feet of hardwood flooring—will make your billing and estimating considerably easier. This is no different than a restaurant menu with established prices for each meal, or an automobile repair shop charging a set amount for an oil change or brake repairs. A lot of your work will lend itself to unit pricing.

Getting Into the Zone

Each of us has a comfort zone, and we tend not to stray too far from it. As the owner of a handyman business, you will stray regularly, at least when you're getting started. You'll find yourself inside strangers' homes, perhaps rooting around under a bathroom sink, learning more than you want to know about the owner's state of health and beauty. There will be pets that trigger allergies, and you might trigger a response in these pets despite an owner's claim that she's never seen Muffy try to bite anyone before.

If you're used to traveling to work by bus or train and like leaving the driving to others, prepare for some commutes that seem to go on forever in suburban subdivisions. And if you're working in urban areas, parking can be time-consuming and inconvenient.

Your financial comfort zone will be challenged, partly by how quickly you're paid by your customers. Most work for small jobs is paid on completion unless you and the customer have made other arrangements or they're on account with you. Other

Taking Parking into Account

Will your business be in some *really* fun city for driving, such as San Francisco or New York? Always ask your customer about parking availability. Preferably, you'll want a driveway, as street parking can be very iffy, especially in neighborhoods requiring residential parking permits for parking over a fixed period of time. When parking is a problem, it eats into your profits and should be calculated into your fees.

times, a bill is sent and final payment could take days (and days). You want your money, but the check is in the mail while you wait. You were never this impatient for your money when you worked for someone else—so what changed?

What changed is that now you have to trust people you don't know to pay you, and this can be unsettling. Don't worry; unpaid bills will be very few and far between, if you have any at all, but there is a certain leap of faith involved (which may be difficult for some).

It's All in the Details

When you're employed by someone else, you never have to deal with a lot of structural details. Office supplies or tools are provided, a management structure often determines your projects and their relative importance, a janitorial service cleans the building, and a uniform service launders your company overalls. You have to show up, intelligently do your job, make some decisions about how to go about it, and go home, sometimes taking work with you. There are dozens of details that are handled by others so you can do your work.

As a handyman, you not only do the actual jobs and attend to those details, but you also have to buy materials and supplies, return customer phone calls, determine a daily schedule (which can change every day), map out the most efficient route for driving, juggle the schedule when a job goes over your estimated time, deposit your payments at the bank, record your activities in your accounting books, keep your tools and equipment in good working order, and then do this, day in and day out.

Details and lists go hand in hand. I always make lists, even in the middle of a repair, if I suddenly think of something I need to do or purchase for a job. You don't need a Blackberry or other electronic recorder—although they're really fun to have— but you do need to keep ongoing, readable to-do or to-buy lists so you don't lose track of jobs, money, and customers. A small notepad and pen in a shirt pocket will do the job—no batteries required, and it won't get damaged if it falls a couple of stories onto a sidewalk.

People Person or Lone Wolf?

Independent, self-employed contractors are just that: independent. They want to live by their own decisions and are not comfortable taking orders or direction from others (even if it's to their benefit—but that's another story). Some of the contractors I've known have been loners who kept their businesses small and only took work they could handle by themselves or with occasional help. They were quite happy spending their days working alone and keeping their own counsel. Others were very gregarious and talked with everyone, but still managed to get their work done in a timely manner.

Either type of person can succeed in the handyman business, but you have to address the type of person you are and attend to your needs at the same time. In fact, you might have a better chance of doing this while running your own business than when working for someone else, where you have little control over your day-to-day environment. As you build up relationships with your suppliers, you'll get to know clerks and managers and owners as camaraderie develops. You'll probably work with real estate agents and property managers, and you may get to know them socially as well. These relationships will not provide the same daily interaction you enjoyed with colleagues when working for a larger company, but they will help ease the transition.

Working Alone

For those who prefer a more private life and work environment, you can specialize in vacant properties, such as apartments that need work done between tenants, or more outdoor work, where you're more likely to work by yourself.

Meet Your New Partner, the Government

You will have a silent partner in this new venture of yours—several, in fact—but they all fall under one umbrella heading: the government. Some would see this as the pernicious evil of Big Brother, while others see it as a generally good thing. I am in the latter category. Without some degree of regulation, we would be living in the Dark Ages, as voluntary self-regulation just doesn't cut it.

What does your new partner want from you? A few things (local regulations might vary):

- You will need to register your business and get a license.
- You will want business insurance, even if it isn't required.
- You should have a surety bond, which provides your customers with limited protection in the event you cause them damages.
- Taxes.

A license says you're a legitimate business, and the state and city know where to find you if they or your customers ever have any problems with you. It normally indicates you have a bond, and insurance as well. If you have an accident on a job, cause injury or damage, and don't have a bond or insurance, your customer could have less recourse to recover damages. And if you're sued and don't have insurance, there will be no end to your financial troubles, as a plaintiff will go after your personal assets. Although unlicensed and uninsured contractors are hired regularly, smarter homeowners won't even consider them, as they're not worth the risk.

Family Life

Working long hours in any job or occupation can take its toll on the individual and on a family. With your new handyman business, you will work long hours, but you'll have the flexibility to work around your kids' schedules and birthday parties and recitals and . . .

Or will you? Once again, it depends.

You might well be tempted to take every job that comes your way, believing each will be the last and you had better grab it while you can. Then another week passes and you start the same routine all over again. What happened to controlling your destiny and making your time your own? It becomes easy to forget those ideals when you're scrambling for money.

The money is important, critical even, but not at any cost. And once your business is established and you're past the paranoia of wondering where your next job will come from, you can ease back and make it to the afternoon soccer games. You can even volunteer as a coach.

It will take some adjusting for you and your family. You might trade off working very late one day so you can stay home the next morning to get the kids off to school, or to attend a parent/teacher meeting. Communication is critical so that everyone understands your work and time at home will be changing, and at times it will be difficult, but not insurmountable. Make some date nights, whether it's a movie and pizza with the kids, or dinner out with your partner.

If communication breaks down, just remember: You're the handyman—you can fix anything.

Now that you've decided the handyman business is for you, it's time to figure out how to make it happen.

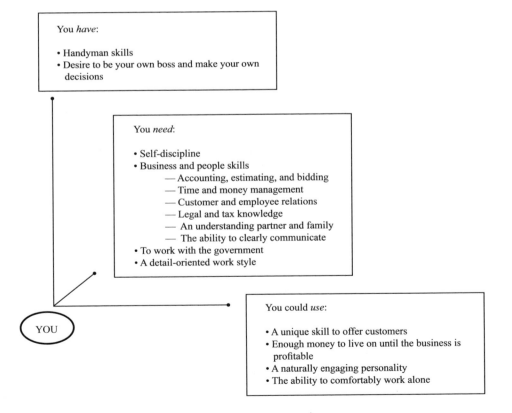

You *have*:

• Handyman skills
• Desire to be your own boss and make your own decisions

You *need*:

• Self-discipline
• Business and people skills
  — Accounting, estimating, and bidding
  — Time and money management
  — Customer and employee relations
  — Legal and tax knowledge
  — An understanding partner and family
  — The ability to clearly communicate
• To work with the government
• A detail-oriented work style

You could *use*:

• A unique skill to offer customers
• Enough money to live on until the business is profitable
• A naturally engaging personality
• The ability to comfortably work alone

YOU

Adjusting Your Rose-Colored Glasses

Envisioning your handyman business is a mental construct of what you want—and hope—your business to be. You bring everything to an imaginary table, lay it all out, and try and separate reality from fantasy (although fantasy can become reality if everything goes well). This is where you weigh your options, pencil out some figures, and try to establish a timeline for your goals. You can be as fanciful as you want with the understanding that immediate gratification will be a bit elusive.

Where do you start? With the basics, of course.

- Is there a local need for another handyman?
- Is there an existing business you want to use as a role model for your business?
- Where do you want to set up your operation?
- How long will this take?
- What will it cost to get started?
- Who is your competition?
- What kind of jobs do you want to do?

Every question will lead to other questions as you brainstorm your way around your new venture. Bring some more brains into the process, especially other small business owners who have gone through this process themselves. You won't think of everything, and the more quality input, the better. Eventually you'll have absorbed enough comments from others and you'll be able to draw your own conclusions. Your vision might change as the realities of the business set in, so flexibility is a must. You might have some initial disappointments, but you could also be so busy from the outset that you'll barely be able to keep up with the work. This is exactly the kind of "problem" most businesses would envy.

Who Needs You?

You're going into this business because it's what you want to do, but is there any need for you? If you're living in a depressed rural area or industrial city that's seen better days, jobs might well be few and far between. How far are you willing to travel to service your future clients? Should you move away altogether?

A high local unemployment rate coupled with a modest-to-low household income suggests your town could have trouble supporting a handyman business. Blue-collar homeowners are less likely to hire a handyman, as they most likely have sufficient repair skills to take care of most maintenance needs. A moderate unemployment rate and a higher range of incomes will more likely welcome a good handyman. A certain critical mass of customers, money, and homes and businesses in need of repairs has to be present for you to have a good chance at success.

Fun Statistics

According to the U.S. Bureau of Labor Statistics (www.bls.gov/):

- There were approximately 5,152,000 installation, maintenance, and repair workers in 2008.
- In the same year, the country had almost sixteen times that number of management, professional, sales, and office workers.
- According to college and career Web site StateUniversity.com (http://careers.stateuniversity.com), in the United States, as per the most recent surveys, there are approximately:

    - 486,000 painters and paperhangers
    - 1.2 million carpenters
    - 500,000 plumbers and pipe fitters
    - 162,000 roofers

Handymen do all of these jobs and more, and the outlook for all six professions is good.

According to Patricia Dinslage of the International Association of Home Business Entrepreneurs:

- Residential improvements and repairs are a $200 billion annual business.
- Seventy-five percent of American homes are over twenty years old.
- Seventy-five percent of American workers are in white-collar professions.
- The population is aging.

What does this mean for you as a handyman?

- Although it's a stereotype, you can expect that fewer white-collar workers will have the time or knowledge to do all of their home maintenance tasks.
- Aging homes and aging owners suggest work needs to be done by owners who are less inclined to do it themselves.
- Americans spend trainloads of money on home improvements.
- You should find plenty of work as a handyman.

The ideal critical mass consists of:

- Wealthy households for whom trusted service and a one-on-one relationship with their contractors is important. These households also expect their contractors to view them with the same degree of importance, meaning their work is scheduled and finished promptly.
- The upper middle class, typically with at least one high income and a homemaker, either full- or part-time, or two reasonably high incomes.
- Professional couples or singles with no time or desire to perform home repairs.
- Retirees with plenty of disposable income.
- Professional clients, including business owners, property managers, and other contractors.

Role Models

If you look to movies for handyman role models, you will find the deranged, the comedic, and the curmudgeonly—entertaining, but not the best examples for your purposes. You don't necessarily need another handyman business to model yours after—unless there's one you happen to admire—but you can look to any small- to medium-size contractor in a similar business, such as painting, janitorial, or carpentry. These businesses will be less varied than yours in their scope of jobs, but will work with a very similar customer base.

A housepainter working alone has to be fairly efficient to be successful. Jobs must be bid, materials ordered and picked up, color samples done for clients, the painting itself finished in a neat and timely manner, the billing prepared, and the fees collected. A good painter will stay busy, but figure out how to schedule enough work ahead without being overwhelmed or putting potential customers off for too long. It's a balancing act well worth observing, as you will go through it yourself.

Self-employed carpenters have to manage long and heavy lengths of lumber alone when they frame room additions or decks. I watched one build a second-story deck by himself, using heavy 6-by-6-inch posts and hauling and installing all the joists, decking, and railing material piece by piece. These were not easy tasks, but over the years he had learned efficient ways to do this work alone. By example, a carpenter such as this one shows you how to adapt to the circumstances of a job without helpers.

Your Headquarters

For most of you, your business will be based out of your home. You'll find a space to set up a small office, or use an existing one, and you'll see if this suits you. Some people have no problem whatsoever working around their partners, kids, and pets, and are able to do their work and not be distracted. (I have a computer systems analyst neighbor who manages this, although I haven't the faintest idea how he does it.) Others would go completely batty and get nothing done.

Bear in mind that you won't need much space for your office, and you can just as easily set yourself up in a garage, attic, or basement and stay away from most distractions. Your office time will be limited, in any case, so your location might not be all that important for you. If you don't like being restricted solely to a home office location, you can always work out of:

- a Starbucks or another coffee joint;
- your vehicle (for a lot of contractors, their vehicle is a portable office); or
- rented shared space.

Some people will never feel their business is the real thing unless they have a destination office space to work out of and commute to. Some property developers have built shared office spaces for just this purpose, where individuals set up shop and rent cubicles or small offices and share common spaces with other small business owners. Rents and expenses vary, and I wouldn't recommend it if you're just starting out, but as your income increases, consider a shared space if the separation between your home and work is important to you. Another option, if you also have limited storage space for tools and materials, is to rent a garage stall or some type of month-to-month mini-storage unit with electrical outlets. Assuming the rental contracts do not bar you from doing occasional office work, this could solve two problems at once without locking you into a long-term lease (your home address or post office box would still be used for business correspondence).

Setting Up Out of Your Home

Be sure you can legally set up your handyman business in your home. Check with your municipality as well as any homeowners association to confirm there are no restrictions.

Time Frame

Once the entrepreneurial bug bites, you'll wish you had started your business the day before and were up and running already. This is normal, but don't quit your day job just yet. Your careful budget and timing projections might prove to be more than a little off the mark (Amazon.com, the Internet retailer, took years before showing a profit).

How long it will take to get up and running will depend on your local economy, the desirability of services you're offering, your fees, and how well you market yourself. By lining up some work in advance—with friends, neighbors, business acquaintances, or relatives—you'll jump-start your business. Another way to get things moving is to start off part-time until your name and reputation are known and referrals start coming in. You could lose some business by not being available full-time, but you must weigh this against the possibility of having too few customers when you first get started. By going part-time, you can test the waters and get established.

Then there is the possibility you'll be busy from the start and never look back. This happened to a French bakery in Seattle, La Boulangerie, the first of its kind in the city, when it opened to a bread-and-pastry-hungry public in the 1980s and began their first day with a line out the door. It's still in business today. A bakery isn't a service business such as yours, but the same principles apply: If the demand exists and you offer quality and reliability, you will succeed.

It Costs How Much?

This is the beauty of the handyman business—the initial costs. Your biggest initial expenditures, aside from your vehicle and tools (which you presumably already own), are the insurance and bond. The fees vary depending on your state and local requirements and the insurance and bonding companies you deal with. Even though you're not doing any structural work or major electrical or plumbing, you are still exposed to risks.

According to Doug Akiyoshi of Quality Risk Management Services, a Mercer Island, Washington, insurance brokerage:

> *Handyman or contract risks in general have become very complex for most insurance companies to underwrite. I know of many insurance agents who still refuse to quote any contracting operations simply because of the amount*

of time and effort involved. Historically, the "handyman" was a skilled individual who performed odd jobs and various small tasks to which there were no defined limitations or restrictions on the type of work performed. As one's skill level progressed, and the potential for significant financial opportunity, many handyman operations gradually evolved into construction-type work. So the term "handyman" is often accompanied with far more questions designed to clearly identify what type of work is being performed.

To insure a true "handyman" operation, it runs $600 to $1,500 annually [use for estimate range only], subject to policy limits, type of license required (specialty or general contractor), contractor work experience, and the type of structures (commercial buildings, tract homes, condos, multifamily, or single family residences) where work is performed.

The annual premium for the bond can run $270 to $1,500 [use for estimate range only], subject to type of license required (specialty or general contractor), which then dictates the bond amount. Ownership of real estate, personal credit history, and financial obligations are all major factors in approval and the pricing of the bond.

One of the first things I advise any contractor (new in business or existing) is to contact the pertinent state agency to determine what classification (general contractor or specialty contractor) is needed for their business. "Handyman services" is generally considered a "catch-all" classification for licensing and insurance purposes, so describing the scope of your contracting operations is almost as important as performing the work itself. Providing general, vague information (i.e., "Well, I might do . . ." or "I'm really not sure . . .") is often interpreted as an individual who may be willing to take on work beyond his expertise, thus higher insurance rates are likely.

Insuring Your Business

Each insurance company will have its own exclusions as to work it will not cover, or will charge higher premiums to cover. My former insurance company would not cover work done with pressure washers, at least when used on buildings, because of the potential for damages, and thus claims. Others might bill higher rates if you expect to be walking around on a roof. Interview several companies and compare their policies before signing up. You should also check your homeowner's policy for coverage of a home office and home storage of tools and materials. Your insurer might require a rider to your standard policy.

Your next biggest expense will be marketing, and that depends on how many ads you run and where you run them. A phone-book ad will cost more than one running in the neighborhood newspaper, for instance.

The SBA

The Small Business Administration (SBA) offers a number of financial assistance programs for small businesses. Go to www.sba.gov/index.html for more information.

Some state programs are also available (see http://usgovinfo.about.com/od/smallbusiness/a/stategrants.htm).

For information on minority and disadvantaged business programs, go to www.ethnicmajority.com/Government_MBE_programs.htm or the Minority Business Development Agency at www.mbda.gov.

Programs aimed at women-owned businesses can be found at www.business.gov/start/woman-owned.

Your Competition—Friends or Foes?

Before starting your business, you'll want to know who else in your area is competing for your potential customers. A quick reading of the Yellow Pages, an online search, and a perusal of local classified ads will give you some idea of how many other handymen, either working on their own or as franchisees of national companies, are in your territory. When there's plenty of work or customers to go around, competition isn't much of an issue (by the way, when a business owner is quoted as saying competition is a good thing, or competition is welcomed, that owner is really, really lying). If things are tight or the local widget factory has layoffs—in which case, you'll find dozens of new, unlicensed handymen, painters, and carpenters running ads and looking for work—you'll have to adjust your business plan in order to compete.

Keep this in mind: Other handymen can be helpful to you. It's a good idea to meet other reliable handymen, see what they specialize in, and exchange business cards. Why? Because there will be times when you're too busy to do a job and will want to recommend someone who can. This in itself is a service, and there's a chance you'll be remembered for it, either by the customer you referred or the handyman who ends up doing the job, which can lead to more referrals for you. Other times a job might require a second body, and you can call on one of your newfound colleagues to give you a hand. Make your competitors your colleagues and you'll all be better off for it.

Working with Competitors

When I would lose a bid to another contractor, I made it a point to call and introduce myself. A few thought this was a bit odd at first, but warmed up after we spoke for a few minutes. I asked if they would please keep me in mind if they were ever bidding jobs that needed a subcontractor for the type of work I did. I ended up working with all of them at one time or another.

Picking and Choosing Your Work

No one can do it all. Regardless of how clever or adaptable you are, you shouldn't do every type of job that comes your way. Handymen, as well as other contractors, get into trouble all the time by claiming they can perform certain tasks only to discover, to the dismay of all parties, that they've made things worse than had they left it alone and called in someone with experience. This doesn't mean you won't learn new things, but choose the time and the place wisely.

Some jobs you simply want to avoid due to personal preference or lack of expertise. You'll lose some bids over it, but you shouldn't lose any sleep. If you're not good with concrete, don't offer to replace missing sections of sidewalk. No chimney-cleaning equipment? Don't pretend you're Bert the chimney sweep from *Mary Poppins*, even if you can sing and dance like Dick Van Dyke. Have a specialty—say, weather-stripping doors? By all means, promote it.

Sticking only with the skills you're good at, on the other hand, can only go so far if this prevents you from offering certain basic handyman services. Great carpentry skills aren't all that helpful if your client has a leaky toilet. Any holes in your work history can be filled through seminars at home improvement stores and community college classes, as well as reading and hands-on practice in your own home.

Wisdom in the handyman business comes, in part, from knowing your best abilities, improving the ones you must, and walking away from the ones you never want to do.

Job Size

Size matters when it comes to your jobs. The bulk of your jobs will be in the low hundreds of dollars, a market that general contractors have little interest in. Why? Given a general contractor's overhead, it's difficult for them to make the desired profit for jobs under a certain dollar amount ($10,000, for instance). A small handyman business can do very well servicing these smaller jobs. Conversely, small companies don't always welcome larger jobs.

Many of the small contractors I've met over the years certainly wanted regular, consistent work, but not necessarily on the same project or building for months and months on end. The notion of returning day after day to the same job, even if it pays well, reminded them too much of "regular" work if it went on for too long. They wanted to bid a job, get it done, and get out. They needed to see the light at the end of the (preferably limited in length) tunnel.

When you envision your business, are you thinking a series of small jobs, say two to four hours each? This means you'll need more customers, which will entail more driving around. It also means, given the time commuting to jobs, that you won't get a full eight hours of on-site work done every day unless you work an extended day. This is one reason you will have to have a minimum charge for showing up.

Are you thinking one day maximum or one day minimum per customer? This can be too restricting. By its very nature, a handyman business will cover two to three jobs a day, including commuting time, and this should be your mind-set. Longer jobs, when you can get them, are a bonus.

Sometimes, you'll start one job only to have it lead to more work on the same job site. Great for you—you want to sell more services—but it can also be frustrating if it means you have to reschedule someone else. Some handymen will take on extensive jobs, such as small bathroom remodels that include coordinating with plumbers and electricians. Does this interest you, or is this more than you can comfortably handle?

Even if a job falls within your expertise, if it's larger than you want to do, be prepared to pass on it. One of the reasons you're choosing self-employment is to do the work you *want* to do and to not get bogged down by work you have no interest in.

Setting a MINIMUM FEE

Don't hesitate to set a minimum fee for your jobs. You can figure, for instance, a minimum of one and a half hours labor plus travel time to get you out the door. Otherwise, you could end up driving longer than it takes to do a job. If a customer balks, turn it around and say there are all kinds of things you can do in that amount of time, if it exceeds how long the initial job requires, including some yard work, gutter cleaning, checking drains, etc. You will lose some jobs with this stance, but you'll be better off for it in the long run. At a very minimum you should bill for a travel charge if a customer decides against you doing a job once you've scheduled to do it and have arrived at the job site.

Do I Have What It Takes (to Get the Job Done)?

You're picturing the type of jobs you want to do; now change the picture. Do you have the tools and equipment to do this work? Is there a disconnect between your vision and what you're actually set up to do?

Here's where you figure out what equipment or additional training you'll need to create the business you want. It might involve a truck (or bigger truck) if you wish to offer hauling services, or a large power tool (a floor polisher, for instance). Any such purchases will affect your budget and planning. Unless you're compelled to offer these services from the start, let them wait until your income will allow for these purchases, or until you have sufficient credit to borrow for them.

Equipment

You don't need to buy new equipment. Clean, well-maintained, used equipment will do the job at a fraction of the cost. Cruise the Internet auction and sales sites for pricing, and then look for sellers close to home. As a handyman, you can always repair used equipment. Another option is renting as needed.

Before investing in any equipment, do some financial projections. Is it really worth spending a few hundred dollars on a sewer snake when most people will call a company that specializes in that kind of work? Maybe it is once word gets around that you do clean-out jobs. Can you ever justify buying and storing scaffolding? Sure, if you do a lot of painting or exterior repairs. Consider starting out with standard handyman jobs first, and then do some market research with your customers. If you conclude there's enough business for you to branch out into additional services, your customers will let you know.

Hitting the Road . . . or Not

You can sell your services anywhere your license allows you to. It's up to you to decide how far you want to drive or otherwise commute to your jobs. I say "otherwise commute" because if you elect to only do simple repairs from a narrowly defined list, and only within walking, bicycling, or public-transportation distance from your home, you can do so with a few tools, easily carried in a backpack. This is very doable; in parts of Asia, tremendous loads are transported on hefty bicycles. You could easily carry hand tools, drop cloths, and even a folding utility chair on the back of a bike or aboard a bus or train.

More likely, you'll be driving (this is America, after all). A lot of time can be spent commuting between handyman jobs, especially if you schedule two or three or more a day. Even if you charge for the time, it can be frustrating. If there's an accident and a road is blocked, your entire schedule will be thrown off, regardless of how carefully you've planned your daily route.

Your new self-employment gives you the opportunity to control your daily driving—unless you restrict yourself to the point of not earning enough money for your needs. A densely populated city will offer plenty of customers within a given radius compared to less-populated areas, and this will, of course, affect your plans. You'll be hitting the road for longer distances in rural Kansas than you would in urban Chicago.

Making Your Lists and Checking Them Twice (or More)

Make a list of your concerns and visions for starting a handyman business. This is a terrific way to help you figure out the direction you want to go in your new career. Your list can be simply a series of questions. Had Napoleon Bonaparte made such a list, he might have stayed out of Russia and occupied himself with turning all of Europe into French suburbs. Instead, he lost almost his entire army as he limped back to Paris in the dead of winter.

Be as inclusive as possible, even if some of your concerns or ideas seem offbeat. If it's important to you to keep showing up for the Wednesday 2:00 AM open-mic amateur comedy spot at Babalou's Pancake Palace, to hone your stand-up skills (and thus putting a damper on getting much handyman work done before noon), so be it. Running your own business gives you opportunities you don't normally get when employed by others, so take advantage of them.

> **Typical List of Concerns and Considerations**
>
> - How much money do I need to earn?
> - How am I going to market myself?
>   - Internet, local papers, or . . . ?
> - How many hours/days a week do I want to work?

- Weekends?
- Evenings?
- Commuting distances: I'm willing to travel _____ miles per day.
- Types of jobs I'm willing to do:
  - Painting and wall repair
  - Deck repairs
  - Minor plumbing (no new pipe installation)
  - Door repairs
  - Minor electrical (replace lights, switches, etc.; no running new wiring)
  - Any yard work or hauling
- Jobs I'll skip:
  - Anything on a roof or higher than two stories
  - Masonry
  - Installing countertops
  - Drain cleaning
- Will I need a truck?
  - If hauling, yes
  - If not hauling, no
- Employees?
  - Maybe
  - Never
- How long do I see myself doing this?
  - 1 to 5 years
  - 5 to 10 years
  - No set time frame

Staffing

Do you want to work alone or with a partner? How about an employee or two, or three? Do you want a partner at home handling the books and the customer calls (this usually means your marital or domestic partner), or one who works side by side with you?

Your life becomes very different when you take on a partner or employee. Few people will do things *exactly* as you would, and you have to learn to accommodate the differences. Others are more than happy to unload the office work onto someone who does it better, allowing the handyman to engage in handy work. I've met very successful couples who run small repair and construction businesses this way.

What about employees? Even if they're family members—sometimes *especially* if they're family members—you'll never be completely satisfied with something (the work itself, the work ethic, personal habits, even their driving). You have to decide if your picky personality can handle the dissonance you'll go through for the benefits of employees.

What are the benefits of having employees?

- You can run multiple jobs at once.
- Someone else does all, or shares in, the physical work.
- The jobs still get done even if you're unavailable.
- More jobs, more income.
- You'll have someone to talk with during the working hours.

Of course, employees bring challenges as well:

- You have to find and interview candidates.
- Dependability is always an issue.
- Training, motivation, and retention required.
- Overhead costs—you will get what, or who, you pay for.
- Personal problems can become work problems.
- It's difficult to find those who share your values.
- You'll have someone who won't stop talking during the working hours.

With just one employee, on most jobs you will end up doing both the work and the supervising. This is a good way for you to clarify whether you want any employees, as well as to develop your skills as a manager. Employees need just that: to be employed. If you work alone, and no work comes up, or you want a day or two off, that's all on you. Employees instantly change that nonchalant attitude, because you must generate enough work for them. Sometimes you'll feel like you're working for your employees instead of the other way around. Not everyone is ready to be a boss or share the business. Part of your envisioning process is to self-examine and decide if this suits you or not.

Employees vs. Independent Contractors

You, as a sole proprietor handyman, are an independent contractor. You cover your overhead, bid your jobs, and submit billings to clients. Even if you found yourself working for one client almost exclusively, you would still be an independent contractor as long as you maintained your own business license, bond, and insurance, and were free to work as a contractor for other clients. There are a lot of advantages to using independent contractors instead of employees: no taxes or withholding to deal with, and very little bookkeeping. An independent contractor will cost more, but if you pass the cost along in your billings and can add on for overhead, and only call a contractor when you need some help, all the better for you.

Given the difference in costs and recordkeeping requirements, some contractors will classify, or attempt to classify, workers as independent contractors, all the while dictating the rate of pay, the work to be performed, and the job hours. An individual cannot be declared an independent contractor if no job independence exists, and all aspects of where, when, and how the work is performed are not within that individual's control. It's a great way to keep your costs down, but it's illegal to declare de facto employees as independent contractors.

This is what the IRS says about independent contractors and employees:

> *In determining whether the person providing service is an employee or an independent contractor, all information that provides evidence of the degree of control and independence must be considered.*

Common Law Rules

Facts that provide evidence of the degree of control and independence fall into three categories:

- Behavioral: Does the company control or have the right to control what the worker does and how the worker works?
- Financial: Are the business aspects of the worker's job controlled by the payer? (These include things like how the worker is paid, whether expenses are reimbursed, who provides tools/supplies, etc.)
- Type of Relationship: Are there written contracts or employee-type benefits (i.e., pension plan, insurance, vacation pay, etc.)? Will the relationship continue, and is the work performed a key aspect of the business?

For more information, refer to Publication 15-A *Employer's Supplemental Tax Guide* (www.irs.gov/pub/irs-pdf/p15a.pdf).

If you want the IRS to determine whether a specific individual is an independent contractor or an employee, file Form SS-8, *Determination of Worker Status for Purposes of Federal Employment Taxes and Income Tax Withholding* (www.irs.gov/pub/irs-pdf/fss8.pdf).

Hiring / Firing / Discrimination Practices

Remember when you were an employee? Remember those laws, posted somewhere in the workplace, stating minimum wage practices and safety rules, and other pertinent information you most likely never read? As an employer, you have to know those laws and follow them to the letter. So much for hiring your cousin for ten dollars an hour and some liquid refreshment . . .

For information on these regulations and how to comply with them, please see appendix A.

THE DREAM

- I'll start making money from day one.
- My customers will love me.
- The jobs will come to me and I'll never want for work.
- When I want a day off, I'll just take it.
- Everything will go like clockwork.
- My days will all be fulfilling.

THE NIGHTMARISH POSSIBILITIES

- The jobs will be few and far between.
- I'll be working so hard just to stay even that I'll never take a day off.
- My customers won't pay on time or their checks will bounce and I'll be out my fees.
- A job will go bad, I'll be sued, and will lose everything, even my CD collection.

THE LIKELY REALITY

- It will take some time to get the business rolling. In the meanwhile, I'll market myself.
- I will eventually be busy enough with normal customers who pay on time without causing me any grief.
- I'll have the occasional bad day, some fantastic days, and a lot of average days, just like most other lines of work.
- When I consider the alternatives, I will be glad I chose to be a handyman.

Customers—The Good, the Bad, and the Ugly

Once you go into business for yourself, the term *customer* takes on a whole new meaning—or, more accurately, several meanings. Now you're the one providing a service that must pass muster with people you've only just met. You must be sufficiently sociable and engaging to convince others of your skills and abilities so they will be comfortable having you into their homes or businesses. You have to trust them enough to pay for your services in a timely manner, hope they'll give you referrals, and call you back for future work. For the most part, nearly all of your dealings with customers will be civil and uneventful.

The key point in successful business dealings with customers is clear and open communication, starting with your first phone conversation. Someone is calling you with a problem and is looking for a solution. You have to convey what you can do, when you can do it, and approximately what it will cost. If any of those conditions change—you find you can't do the job, your schedule changes, the price goes up because the job is more complicated than you expected—you must tell your client this as soon and as clearly as possible. We tend to be more understanding of bad news if we hear it in a timely and fully explained manner rather than hearing vague musings or nothing at all.

On the other hand, some people don't want to hear anything bad or unexpected, and you'll have to learn to deal with them as well. Your goal is a satisfied customer who becomes a repeat customer.

Is There Any Such Thing as the Perfect Customer?

For the most part, your vision of content, satisfied customers is justified. Most *will* be content and satisfied if you do your job well. Customers, like all people, fall into several broad categories, and you'll need to adjust and adapt to all of them, including those who say things such as:

- "How can such a small job take so long?"
- "Well, it wasn't exactly what I was expecting, but I guess it will do."
- "Oh, I guess I should have cleared all this stuff out of your way first, huh?"
- "I didn't think the paint color would be this dark. Can you lighten it up before it dries?"

Some customers will greet you with open arms and an offer of breakfast. Others will be at work and leave a key for you, asking that you lock up when you're finished.

A (merciful) few will sit and watch the entire time you work (this can be unnerving, as I discovered when half the tenants of a small apartment house individually stayed in the rooms I was working in for hours on end, just staring). Occasionally, someone will want you to show them how to do the repairs while you're doing them, explaining each step. This is fine if you signed on as a tutor, but otherwise, any lengthy instruction will eat into your repair time.

For some customers (and their kids and pets), you'll be a source of fascination, which can lead to a welcome amount of respect for your work, or a million questions and offers of coffee every ten minutes. You will have to tactfully press on without offending.

It All Starts at the Front Door

Before arriving at a customer's house or business, it would be to your advantage to send out a brochure or flyer introducing yourself and listing all the jobs you do. This provides some background and a sense of legitimacy. That said, your customer's first visual impression of you really counts. You have to take this into consideration as you plan your business. You might see old clothes and ripped jeans as a sign of someone who's really working and gets the job done. Your customer sees someone who can't afford decent clothing and then thinks twice about choosing you for the job.

How do you want to present yourself?

- Do you envision company work shirts with your name printed on them?
- Matching overalls for employees?
- Regardless of how superficial you might consider fashion and clothing to be, appearances matter.

How you speak or articulate is also important, especially if English isn't your primary language. Your customer wants to be assured you understand each other, and the onus is on you to make this happen. Fair or not, you don't want your intelligence or ability to perform to be based strictly on a perceived language or educational barrier. Do you think this will be an issue for you? A great show of self-confidence and an outgoing personality can overcome some language difficulties, but if you're the more retiring type who can read English better than speak it, consider writing out some standard customer presentations and practicing them orally. This gets your foot in the door where your good work should speak for itself.

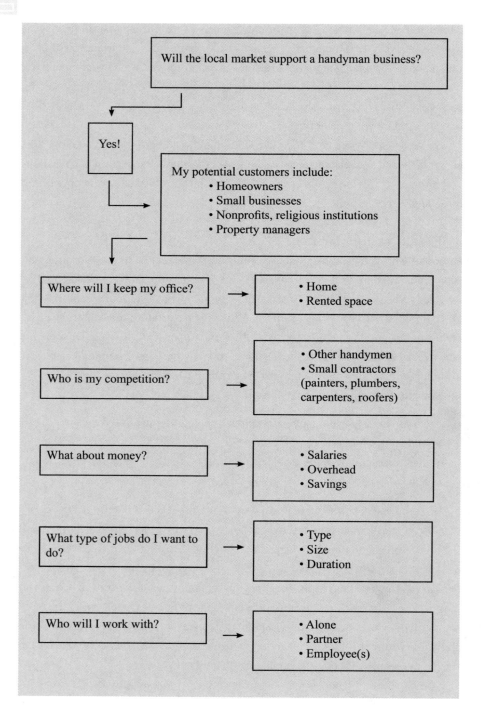

Will the local market support a handyman business?

Yes!

My potential customers include:
• Homeowners
• Small businesses
• Nonprofits, religious institutions
• Property managers

Where will I keep my office?
→
• Home
• Rented space

Who is my competition?
→
• Other handymen
• Small contractors (painters, plumbers, carpenters, roofers)

What about money?
→
• Salaries
• Overhead
• Savings

What type of jobs do I want to do?
→
• Type
• Size
• Duration

Who will I work with?
→
• Alone
• Partner
• Employee(s)

Once You're Inside . . .

It takes a certain level of trust for your customer to give you access to a house or place of business. You don't want to do anything to bring that trust into question. This means that not only your own behavior must be impeccable, but also that of any employees. If you don't feel comfortable hiring people for this level of responsibility, it will affect the size of your business and the types of jobs you do, as you will stay limited to those you can do alone unless you hire another licensed contractor as needed.

First Customer Contact—A Journey into the Unknown

When a potential customer calls, your sales persona must take over. You have to sell yourself and your ability to solve a repair problem competently, at a competitive price, and in a timely manner. You also have to communicate the terms by which you operate.

Handyman: Hello, this is Hannibal's Home Repair. How may I help you?

Caller: Yes, hello. I have a leak under my kitchen sink. Is this something you can repair?

Handyman: Yes, ma'am, I do all types of plumbing repair. Can you tell me if the leak occurs only while the water is running, or does it leak after the water is shut off?

Caller: Well, I really didn't notice.

Handyman: All right. Is there a dishwasher? Does it leak when the dishwasher is running?

Caller: It seems to leak all the time.

Handyman: Okay, it sounds like it's the faucet, although it could also be the drain line. I can repair either one.

Caller: Oh, that's great! When can you come out?

Handyman: I can be there on Friday, about mid-afternoon. Does that work for you?

Caller: Yes, I'll be here.

Handyman: Fine. I can give you an estimated price now. Unless some unusual conditions are present, this will be your cost. I will inspect the job first before doing any work. I do add a travel charge which covers my travel time to your home. I will bring a short contract outlining the work and present it to you for a signature. Afterward, I'll do the repairs to your satisfaction and present your billing. Payment will be due at that time. In the meanwhile, I will mail or e-mail you a company brochure outlining the other services I offer, in case you need anything else done now or in the future. The brochure also states my contracting license number as well as noting that I am insured and bonded. Does this work for you?

Caller: Why, yes, that sounds very satisfactory. So, what will this cost?

Handyman: My travel charge is $35. The repair should run somewhere between $50 and $75, including materials. While I'm there, I'll check your dishwasher connection as well. If for any reason the faucet itself is beyond reasonable repair and needs replacement, I'll show you a selection of faucets I can order and will not charge an additional travel fee when I come to install the new faucet. I do ask that you clean out the area under the sink so I can get right to the job and not have to bill time for my cleaning it out. I will call you Thursday night to confirm our appointment, and will see you on Friday.

Caller: All right, then; thank you very much.

Handyman: Thank you. I appreciate the call.

How did Hannibal handle this call? He asked for a description of the problem, did a quick diagnosis, and figured it could be one of two or three possibilities. He stated his fees and terms, made an appointment, and said he would send out a brochure listing his services. He said he would confirm the appointment the night before, and asked if these terms were satisfactory to the customer. When he arrives at the job site, he'll have a prepared contract that describes the job, ready for the customer to sign *before* he begins the repairs. His clear communication is both to his and the customer's benefit.

Value of a Business Binder

A good marketing tool is a business binder containing company background information, a copy of your license, bond, and insurance, a price list, a list of all your services, photos of your work, and testimonial letters from past customers. A separate product book with information and marketing material on all the products you install can also boost sales.

Your business vision should assume the possibility of some breakage or damages as you work in occupied buildings. Tools fall, vases knock over, and paint spills. Accidentally or not, you'll be responsible. The condition of the areas you work in will affect your bidding, and is something you should consider now. A room full of antique furniture and Oriental rugs will require more finesse and concern than an empty garage with a concrete floor. Finesse means more time, and that means more money. Don't assume every job will have a cleared path and easy access.

Bidding Options for Customers

When carpet installers bid a job, they charge extra for moving any furniture out of the way. Empty rooms, of course, are easiest to bid and the least expensive for the clients. You should let a client know in advance that you will have to bill for time spent providing access to perform a job if there are too many obstacles in the way. This gives the customer the option of clearing out the work area or paying you to do it.

Put It on My Tab

Cash flow is one chamber of the heart of every business. You'll have to decide your payment policy before you start any actual jobs. What are your options?

- Payment upon completion
- Down payment (for materials, or materials and part of the labor) in advance, and the balance due when the job is finished
- Progress billings
- Bill at the end of the job, and payment due in five to seven days (or more)

Payment upon completion is the standard for handyman jobs. You finish, you present the bill, and you receive a payment. It's quick, simple, and there's no waiting for a check. For jobs requiring a sizable outlay for materials (gallons of paint, boxes of tile, a truck full of lumber, etc.), it's appropriate to get a down payment up front for the materials. This protects you in the event a customer doesn't pay for the job in a timely manner (or at all); at least you won't be out the cost of the materials.

On larger, lengthier jobs—and you'll have to define these terms for yourself—progress payments, say, every one or two weeks, is a standard practice (on very large jobs and with general contractors, these payments are monthly). The least-appealing option is leaving or sending a billing statement and waiting for a return payment by mail. *Never start a job without defining the terms of payment first!*

Business Binder and Product Book

A business binder, which you present to clients, should contain the following:

- Background information on you and the company
- Copy of your business license
- Copy of your certificate of insurance
- Copy of your bond
- Blank contract and estimate forms
- Receipts

- Change order forms
- List of all your services
- Price list for standard services
- Photos of past jobs
- References
- Any testimonial letters from past customers
- Organization memberships (e.g., Better Business Bureau)

A product book should contain marketing materials for products you install and use, including:

- Storage systems
- Door locks
- Weather stripping
- Electrical fixtures (fans, lights, doorbells)
- Plumbing fixtures
- Shower doors
- Cabinetry
- Paints and finishes
- Decking
- Garage door openers
- Windows and screens
- Flooring
- Vanities
- Tile and countertops

Setting Up a Merchant Account

Consider setting up a merchant account at any number of banks or other providers, enabling you to accept credit cards, which makes sense in an almost totally plastic money world. You will get paid faster and avoid any problems with bounced checks. Depending on the fee per transaction (assume 3 percent), you might consider building transaction costs into your own fees if you end up with a lot of credit card payments. That said, Regulation CC (Expedited Funds Availability) of the Federal Reserve mandates that most local checks under $5,000 (within the same check-processing region as your bank) be cleared within two business days of deposit. See www.buyerzone.com/finance/credit_merchants/buyers_guide2.html for more information.

Remember, cash isn't just king, it's the entire royal family—including the inbred, nitwit cousins. To keep money as familial as possible, be sure to establish payment-on-completion terms up front before starting your jobs.

Writing a Business Plan

You've given the handyman business a lot of thought, and now you're ready to do it. You've designed the company logo in your head, and you're planning what to serve at your launch date party. All that's missing is a business plan.

Great, you say. This is just like your mother telling you to bundle up and put on your coat, boots, and gloves before running outside after the first winter snow, the one that just closed your school. You can't wait to get out and start throwing snowballs. Who wants to write up a plan? You've got faucets to repair and caulk to buy and customers to meet.

A business plan is one of those nagging necessities that force you to examine your assumptions, your ideas, and your strengths and weaknesses. Some self-examination up front can save a lot of heartache later. Vision guides—the plan helps decide. Think of writing the plan as proving you have the self-discipline to start up and run your new business. (Yes, that's probably something your mother would say, but you have to admit—she was right about a *few* things.)

Your plan will outline what you want to do, how you expect to do it, and provide a time frame for accomplishing your business goals. It isn't set in stone—it will evolve—but an initial plan provides much needed guidance and support. It will help you avoid expensive pitfalls—although not necessarily all of them (there are no guarantees with a business plan)—and keep you on track.

We Want to See Your Plans . . .

A business plan isn't just for you. Any bank or other lender you negotiate with for a business loan will want to know your plans. For one thing, they'd like to know how you intend on paying them back (lenders being somewhat fussy about these things).

Business Plan 101

Don't know what a business plan looks like? Need some hints? Go to www.sba.gov/smallbusinessplanner/plan/writeabusinessplan/index.html and let the Small Business Administration (SBA) provide you with samples and plenty of other advice for new business owners.

Have you done any market research or figured out how to sell your handyman service? A business plan will help guide that as well. Marketing throws many new, and established, business owners for a loop—a big loop. Even experienced companies have notable failures. (Remember New Coke? You don't? There's a reason.) Simply saying you'll go forth and fix the world isn't enough. You have to define that world and connect with its inhabitants. If this part of your business plan stymies you, that's a good thing. It means you have a problem to solve before you go any further.

Business Plans are Essential

Think of your business plan as a set of assembly instructions. Like any instructions, skip or compromise a step and the final product might not look like or work the same as the picture on the box. Formulating your plan can feel like nuisance work—do it anyway to avoid the regrets of not doing it.

Business plans are pretty basic regardless of the nature of the enterprise. You describe, outline, and explain what you intend to do as though you're addressing a complete stranger who must come away with a clear understanding of your enterprise. If writing and cogitating about such things isn't your strong suit, there's free help available from those in the know—retired business managers who have been where you're trying to go.

Former Execs to the Rescue

The Service Corps of Retired Executives goes by the handy acronym SCORE. Who are they? Allow their Web site—www.score.org/index.html—to do the talking:

> *SCORE: Counselors to America's Small Business is a nonprofit association dedicated to educating entrepreneurs and the formation, growth and success of small business nationwide. SCORE is a resource partner with the U.S. Small Business Administration (SBA).*
>
> *SCORE is headquartered in Herndon, VA, and Washington, DC, and has 389 chapters throughout the United States and its territories, with 10,500 volunteers nationwide. Both working and retired executives and business owners donate time and expertise as business counselors. SCORE was founded in 1964.*
>
> *We are America's premier source of free and confidential small business advice for entrepreneurs.*
>
> *SCORE services won't cost you anything but your time. You'll get solid advice, some of which you might not want to hear because it doesn't match your ideas. Keep an open mind about it, as this advice can save you some grief and expense.*
>
> *Part of being an entrepreneur is believing more in yourself than others do, following a vision without hesitation, and living the dream. That's great, but visions are not flawless, and they can also be blinding. Listening to some feedback and challenging some of your assumptions will make you a better business owner.*

Score

SCORE's "Our Sponsors" Web site page (www.score.org/alliances.html) offers some excellent nonprofit links for new business owners. These sites include questionnaires, newsletters, and resources geared to small businesses. They also offer business plan templates and other business-related templates at www.score.org/template_gallery.html.

Business Plan Basics

A basic business plan should include:

- Executive Summary or Overview
- Who you are
- What you intend to do
- What your business owns
- Who it anticipates as customers
- Company Description
- Short history of you and your background
- Current status
- Marketing and Promotion
- Market research
- Describe how and where you're marketing the business
- Promotional materials
- Organization and Management
- Partners or co-owners
- Number of employees and their positions
- Temp workers
- Proposed Services and Products
- List the types of work you plan on doing
- If you expect to sell any products (cleaners, tools, etc.), list those
- Legal description
- Sole proprietor, partnership, incorporated, etc.
- Proposed method of operation
- Describe how you will deliver your services
- A typical day
- Procuring materials
- Commuting
- Goals and time frame for meeting them
- Financial expectations
- Expanding your staff

- Where you will be in 12 months, 24 months, etc.
- Financial information
- Current financial assets
- Loans against the business

Explain Yourself

You might not be requiring any outside funding and be tempted to skip writing a business plan. Remember, it's as much a guide for you as a snapshot for others. There will be times when you're at a crossroads with your business and will want to refer to your original vision as outlined in the plan. Also, if expansion is a possibility and a loan is needed later, your plan will be finished and only in need of some updating.

The initial sections of your business plan can be used as background information for a Web site or for bidding contract jobs. For instance, you might bid to service the various buildings for a property manager who wants to know something about you. The same information can be given to local newspaper reporters writing up a piece on your new business (neighborhood publications like good filler material and do this regularly).

The Dreaded Marketing

Marketing is not the favored activity of small businesses. You're a handyman; you want to fix things and make improvements, not be bothered with an advertising campaign. Ralph Waldo Emerson said, "Build a better mousetrap and the world will beat a path to your door." That was barely true in the nineteenth century when he wrote it, and it certainly isn't true in an age of YouTube, nonstop cable TV, and iPhones. Even a better mousetrap needs to be marketed, and so do you—at least when you're getting started.

Ask yourself these questions:

- To whom are you marketing?
- Who needs a handyman?
- Who do you want as customers?

You see the local condo market as a perfect target for your services, but until you do some market research, you won't ever discover that this market is already fully serviced by a competitor who is deeply entrenched with every condo manager in town, and isn't especially interested in sharing the business with you. This is where the telephone is your friend as you prepare a pitch and an inquiry to these same managers, to test the waters. Maybe they would love to have someone like you available for handyman jobs, or maybe they're already fully served, thank you very much. Find out first and adjust your target customers accordingly.

The Campaign

You're a handyman, so your advertising campaign will be somewhat limited. No need to hire a film crew or marketing director, but do consider any and every free opportunity to get your name out to the public. Aside from the usual flyers, business cards, and local ads (please see chapter 5), consider:

- Offering your services at a charity auction or a park clean-up day—any public function that would provide some exposure and an opportunity to pass out some promotional materials is a good bet.
- Have some T-shirts printed with your company name and logo, and wear one as often as possible.
- Get a sign with the company name and phone number to attach to your vehicle.
- Order some inexpensive yard signs to place outside while you're on the job.
- Use youtube.com, myspace.com, and other networking sites—you can even post instructional videos.
- Become your own pitchman by developing a persona for video and print ads.

Get It on Paper

Personally, I feel a little dubious about using printed flyers and brochures as *primary* marketing materials. So few offer any visual or informational appeal, and I suspect most go straight to the recycling bin. In your business plan, figure on spending some real design time with your paper advertising. Consider your own reaction to flyers you find on your door or in the mail. The ones you read and keep are the ones that stand out or happen to be timely in meeting a need.

Trademark Your Business

You can trademark your business name and logo or other design element with the United States Patent and Trademark Office (www.uspto.gov/) for $325. You must do some research to confirm your proposed trademark isn't already in use, or you can pay an intellectual property search firm to make this determination. Some firms will also register your trademark for you. The Patent and Trademark Office offers research databases and information for conducting your search.

Do you have any community access cable channels that feature home repairs? See if you can appear as a guest speaker. Better yet, any local home and garden shows welcome guests with special talents or expertise (be sure to wear your company T-shirt). We live in an age of exaggerated media influence, so take advantage of it. For more on marketing, please see chapter 10.

Get Your Name Out There

It is illegal to leave flyers and brochures in mailboxes. Only stamped and delivered items can be placed in mailboxes, and then only by employees of the U.S. Postal Service. You are also prohibited from attaching anything to the outside of a private mailbox. Yes, it happens all the time, but it only takes one complaint to cause you some trouble.

You might keep a menu from a favored take-out restaurant, but advertising for cleaning services, landscaping, and so on often get tossed. Consider your points of distribution in your business plan. Make an arrangement to leave brochures and business cards with local hardware stores at the same time you place doorknob hangers—those cardstock advertisements that get hung on entry doorknobs—at hundreds of homes.

Organization and Management

If your business is only you, your organization chart will be the simplest one imaginable: just write your name in all of the boxes. Employees, partners (silent and active), and investors all need to be accounted for, however. Writing up your plan gives you time to contemplate hiring employees (full-time or temporary), and ascertaining the costs and benefits. You might envision a dozen trucks and a score of employees. Fine; put them in your plan and see how they pencil out. Once you see the numbers in front of you, you may decide that hiring temps when you need them is more cost-effective.

This is what your business plan does for you: It provides the start of a reality check, which will be confirmed later when you estimate the costs and returns of your fabulous ideas. You can implement some ideas immediately, while others will get tucked away until your business grows enough to accommodate them. Just looking at an org chart full of employees and managers and supervisors might act as a sufficient warning that this isn't the kind of business you aspire to have.

Off to Work You Go

You're a handyman, so you can do anything—or can you? Even if you can, *should* you? Your business plan should list the major categories of service you expect to offer. Why? Because what you offer to do affects your tools and materials budget, the type of vehicle you drive, and the length of individual jobs. It takes considerably longer to drywall a ceiling than it does to replace a faucet washer, for instance. With your jobs and services list staring you in the face, you can whittle it down or, if it appears too short and limiting, add to it to assure you're versatile enough to stay busy.

Sample List

Carpentry

Deck repairs

Repair loose floorboards

Install interior trim

Trim doors

Window repairs

Painting

Interior

Exterior

Floors

Decks

Light prep work only (no stripping)

Refinishing

Touch-up

Miscellaneous

Floor buffing

Trash hauling (no appliances)

Lock replacement

Install weather stripping

General clean-up

Plumbing

Install fixtures

Repair toilets

Repair leaky faucets

Install new faucets

Drain cleaning

Exterior Work

Clean and patch gutters and downspouts

Wash windows

House washing

Power-wash driveways, sidewalks, and decks

Lawn mowing

General gardening

Patch composition roofing

Electrical

Replace switches and receptacles

Replace light fixtures

Install ceiling fans (wiring must be pre-installed)

Install garage door openers (wiring must be pre-installed)

Is this list too ambitious? Not inclusive enough? This is the time to give it some thought, *before* you begin advertising and designing marketing materials. Interior and exterior painting look all-inclusive—do you really want to do jobs that big? Can you compete with landscape companies on lawn-mowing prices? Probably not, so why try—unless you're offering it as a convenience to a customer who just might need it done while you're working on another task. If that's the case, you might consider a section of optional type work, with an explanation that you are available to do these types of jobs if needed, but they are not your mainstay.

Selling Trinkets

I don't know who originated the term revenue streams, but your handyman business offers you opportunities for more than one source of income, and you should consider these in your business plan. These are in addition to any fixtures or materials that are included as part of your jobs. For instance, you can sell:

- commercial cleaning supplies;
- your own written and printed maintenance guides and booklets;
- weather stripping and hardware, which you purchase wholesale, for those clients who want to install it themselves;
- any related items you might find in bulk at auctions (hand tools, for instance); and
- items you create and build, such as picnic tables, birdhouses, toy chests, or wood planters.

I wouldn't suggest you make any of these items the focus of your handyman business, of course, but if you find customers regularly in need of or requesting such items, then investigate the sales possibilities.

You can also sell maintenance contracts. As an example, for a monthly fee, a client could buy a few hours of your time to perform general maintenance, perhaps at a reduced rate. This might appeal to owners of apartment complexes who often have repair lists due to multiple tenants. If you live in an area with vacation homes or cabins, you could offer a winter/spring service (shutting off water before freezing weather sets in, draining water heaters, checking for nesting critters in the spring). Consider any and all possibilities and include them in your plan.

Will they all work out? No; but this is a good time to let your imagination roam, since they require only a small monetary outlay, if any.

According to the Law . . .

Do you know how to legally define your business? You have several choices:

- Sole proprietorship
  - You're it—the boss, the one who earns and keeps all the money.
  - All decisions are yours.
  - All the debts and liabilities are yours.
  - It's the simplest and most common form of small businesses.
- Partnership
  - Profits and liabilities are shared by more than one person.
  - It's important to spell out responsibilities and percentage of ownership.
  - You can be responsible for your partner's business debts.
  - Disputes among partners are not uncommon.
  - It can be a problem if one partner wants out.
- Corporation
  - This is a separate entity with its own rights and responsibilities.
  - Owners are not personally liable for the corporation's debts.
  - This type of business is easily sold.
  - It entails taxation (corporate taxes and individual taxes due) and complexity issues.
- Limited Liability Company (LLC)
  - Like a corporation, an LLC is a separate entity, offering liability protection for its owner(s).

- There are no corporate taxes for LLCs, only individual taxes (taxed like a sole proprietorship or partnership).
- Setting up and maintaining an LLC is a more complicated venture than a sole proprietorship.

It's safe to say you are most likely going to choose a sole proprietorship, at least when you first open your new handyman business. As your company grows, you can revisit the different types of ownership.

Starting Up

It takes money to make money, and starting a handyman business is no exception. You need tools, license, insurance, bond, transportation, and so on, but you also need money to live on while you get your business up and running. *Be realistic in figuring your start-up costs and the discontinuation of income from your former employment!*

Seeing this in front of you in your business plan can be very sobering. You not only have to prepare to get by for the first month or so on a reduced income—but you might have to get by for *several* months, depending on the market and other factors previously discussed.

Consider your best- and worst-case scenarios:

- How many expenses are you willing to reduce or eliminate for six months ?
- How long can you go until your savings and anticipated revenue will cut you short?
- What's your comfort level?

You know what your fixed expenses are; now calculate in some emergencies—a new water heater, a major car repair, plane tickets home when someone becomes gravely ill. You don't have to figure in every possible emergency—you would never have enough money—but some plausible ones. Then look at all the numbers (see chapter 4) and decide how much time you'll need, or are willing to take, to get this new enterprise off the ground.

Fixed Costs, Variable Costs, and Estimated Fees

Your fixed costs will be easy enough to estimate—so much per year for insurance, so much for a bond and license renewals. Variable costs are a bit trickier, but not impossible to estimate for the purposes of your business plan. You'll have vehicle costs—fuel, repairs, insurance, depreciation, payments, if any—which can be found online at any number of Web sites (e.g., www.edmunds.com/apps/cto/CTOintro Controller). Your costs will vary depending on your circumstances, but these sites provide an approximation usable for your business plan.

Advertising and marketing expenses can be estimated based on the cost of a phone-book ad for a given size, newspaper ads, or the cost of a Web site. An initial order of business cards, flyers, and brochures is a very small item, so you can calculate in a fixed amount (say $100 to $200) for enough to get you started.

Will you need more tools? Which ones? Prices are available online or by taking a walk through your nearest home improvement store. You can come up with usable, approximate costs for pretty much all your variable items (you can always throw in a fudge factor as well).

The total of your regular, ongoing costs equals your overhead. This is a critical number because you need to figure it in with all your billings. If your overhead averages out to $150 a week, for instance, your daily overhead cost is $30 based on a five-day work week, and you will charge for this either in your hourly rate, which is most common, or as a separate item, which is far less common.

Now, what about your fees?

Figuring Fees

There are a number of printed books and software programs available, by industry, which offer guides for estimating the costs of just about any type of building or repair job. Unit costs, square footage costs, along with adjustments for different labor rates (they vary all over the country) offer more exacting alternatives than merely eyeballing a job and coming up with a price.

Estimating Costs

One major book publisher is R. S. Means. Home Tech Online (www.hometech online.com) is a big believer in bringing the handyman and other construction-related businesses into the twenty-first century by applying disciplined business techniques and accounting measures. Their book, *HomeTech's 2009 Handyman Cost Estimator* (www.hometechonline.com/handyman/default.htm) offers sample pages for free viewing prior to purchasing the book.

But is this overkill for a handyman?

Your fees will be based on:

- the amount of time you take to complete the job;
- the cost of the materials plus any markup;
- your overhead; and
- any additional profit you add in (some businesses figure their profit into the hourly rate or combine it with the overhead).

Once you've established an hourly rate, plugging the figures in is pretty simple.

Example

Paint one bedroom: five hours @$45/hr, or $225

Materials (paint, caulk, fillers, sandpaper, etc.): $75

Overhead: $35

Profit: 10 percent of job total, or $33.50

Estimated cost: $368.50

Is this price too high? Too low? It depends on the cost of the materials, the prep and cleaning time, the amount of woodwork, and a host of other variables. Painters who specialize in vacant apartments might charge by the square foot or the number of bedrooms, but they offer these prices for a very basic job and materials, with disclaimers that the prices apply to "modern, standard-size" apartments, with "wood windows extra."

A more exacting figure would go by the:

- square footage of the bedroom;
- number of doors;
- number of windows; and
- lineal feet of molding and trim.

By now, you've done enough different jobs to have a good idea how much time is involved to complete certain tasks. The key difference is you must now establish an hourly rate and figure in your overhead and profit when estimating a job. For the sake of your business plan, you need to establish these figures and include every cost you expect to incur, from travel time to time spent estimating jobs and speaking with clients over the phone. It all adds up, and unlike your former jobs where you were paid for all your working hours, self-employment demands more of your time at all hours. You should not go without compensation, so make it part of your overhead (please see chapter 4).

If, after you've become established, you decide your rates are too low (or too high if you're not getting enough work due to your higher bids), you can always change them and recalculate. Assumptions change, and you should be flexible enough to change with them.

Setting Rates

The U.S. Department of Labor (www.dol.gov) and nongovernment Web sites such as PayScale (www.payscale.com) offer regional average surveyed wages for carpenters, painters, and other professions, which can help guide your own rates.

For more discussion on business costs and fees, please see appendix B.

Plan B

It sounds awfully pessimistic to consider what to do if your best-laid plans don't work out, but it's better to be prepared and ready to adjust to whatever reality comes your way. As I write this, the country is in, by the estimation of more than a few economists, the worst financial crisis since the Great Depression. Sturdy businesses with wonderful credit scores, little if any debt, and no seeming connection to the causes of our current problems are finding their revenues greatly reduced as wallets and pocketbooks stay firmly shut. You could open your business during the height of prosperity and still run into a rough patch through no fault of your own (illness could strike you or a family member, a natural disaster could occur, a business partner could raid the company bank account). A backup plan gives you some breathing room and an opportunity to regroup and start again. It might mean going back to work for someone else or changing the types of jobs you're doing (taking on more painting, for instance).

An alternative plan can also consider another scenario: more jobs than you can handle from the very start. Now you have to start thinking about employees, training, more vehicles, and more time spent estimating jobs to keep you and your staff busy.

Use your business plan to outline what you'll do in either case.

More planning, you say? I *still* want to get out and start pounding nails and patching walls.

Yes, you do, but if the money doesn't work out regardless of your best projections, then the handyman business isn't for you. It *should* work out; the work pays handsomely in the right markets. Doing some financial planning is no different than figuring out whether you can afford a certain house or not. You look at the price, the terms, and the expected expenses, and compare them to your current income. If you can't cover the costs, you back away and find something less expensive. Right now, your current expenses—what you spend to maintain your lifestyle, even at a minimum—have to be met by your handyman income. If your projections, even the optimistic ones, can't meet those expenses, you should reconsider being a handyman at this time.

The Big-Ticket Items

Your biggest single ongoing expense will be you and your salary.

- How much do you need to earn to meet your expenses?
- How much do you want to earn to claim success?

At first, keeping current with your bills and taxes might be enough, but you'll want to go beyond this. Otherwise, what's the point of running the business? If you're only getting by, how long are you willing to do so? Six months? A year?

It's an important consideration. New business owners realize it takes time to build up a clientele and start making some real money. Restaurant owners are especially aware of this, and take out large loans or procure money from partners or investors to open up everything from a chili parlor to an elegant night spot. You have to decide how long you want to live with what might be a limited income.

Be realistic in your salary needs. If your fixed personal and business costs are $3,000 a month before taxes, then you'll want to earn at least this much, unless you want to live partially on savings. Living on savings means planning ahead so you have enough stashed away to allow your handyman business enough time to develop and grow.

Hired Help

Employees are next up on your expense sheet. You'll have to decide on an hourly rate and whether you want someone—or more than one—part-time or full-time. Each employee comes with a tax burden (see chapter 8) and overhead costs. If you pay too little, your help will be less than dependable (you often do get what you pay for). A fair and reasonable salary could be beyond your reach, at least at first, unless the employee is generating money for you. Some handymen want to take on large jobs right from the start and will figure on hiring staff, while others want to start slow and test the waters. Decide which handyman you are and stick with your convictions. You can always hire help later on as your business thrives.

Open Your Checkbook

Let's start with your most expensive non-personnel purchases, one of which is a vehicle. The size and type strictly depend on the work you intend on doing, but you have a lot of options.

Americans have been sold on trucks. According to the *Los Angeles Times*, we purchased more light trucks (a category that includes pickups, SUVs, and minivans) for most of the decade prior to 2008 than we purchased passenger cars. Money was cheap and so was fuel, but no longer. You have to be smarter with your money and not overspend on a truck you don't necessarily need.

Hand tools, power tools, and ladders can be easily transported using most passenger cars (a roof rack can accommodate multiple ladders). Hatchback models with fold-down seats are especially adaptable if you need to carry lumber or other long items.

If you must have a truck or van to replace your current vehicle, consider something used. Every car and truck is subject to depreciation or loss in value due to age, popularity (or lack thereof), quality issues, and myriad other factors. New vehicles typically lose the most dollar value since their purchase prices are normally the highest they'll ever be. Why take the hit? You need a dependable, clean vehicle that makes you money instead of costing you money.

You're a handyman; you don't need a shiny new half-ton pickup. However, your customer doesn't want to see you drive up in a rusting, smoking wreck, either, because, fair or not, it brings up questions of your reliability.

Getting Around

I carried all of my tools and ladders with a Volkswagen Rabbit hatchback for seven years and never had any problems. It was cheap, compact, and did the job. I purchased the Rabbit when it was two years old for a grand total of $4,000. It carried a 32-foot extension ladder along with a 12-foot stepladder on its roof rack. *Every* other contractor I knew drove a truck or a van whether they needed one or not.

Vehicles depreciate and new ones eat up money that's better spent elsewhere. If you find an older model that's mechanically fine, but needs a paint job, then haul out your brush, foam roller, or sprayer and paint it (there are plenty of online instructions for painting your own car). This is what a handyman does—and think of the money you'll save.

Insurance

Your vehicle will need to be insured, but this isn't all the insurance you'll need. In addition, you'll need coverage on the business itself, and you should think about medical and disability insurance for yourself as well, if you're not covered by a partner's policy. Why disability? Now that you're about to go out into the business world on your own, you'll have no employer-supplied insurance of any kind unless you provide it, since you're now your employer. It's easy to take insurance coverage for granted, but if you get injured on a handyman job, your income drops to zero.

The first person you should talk with about any medical or disability insurance is the broker or agent who handles your automobile and/or home insurance policies. Your current insurance carrier might not carry either of these policies, but you would be pointed in the right direction. A good online source for price comparisons is www.ehealthinsurance.com. Note that this isn't an endorsement; just use it as a starting point. The world of health insurance is a byzantine one, and there are a lot of variables involved, including your age, health status, personal habits, and the risks associated with your work (a trapeze artist will probably pay more than a librarian, all other things being equal).

Vehicle Insurance

Ask your state licensing agency or insurance commission about any mandatory insurance you must carry to do business in your area. This is especially true if you have any employees. For a list of all state insurance commissioners, go to www .naic.org.

Disability

If you're unable to work, a disability policy will cover a portion of your lost income, usually to a maximum of 80 percent. These benefits are tax-free to you as long as you are the one paying the premiums. The stipulations of these policies—for both long-term and short-term disability insurance—differ as to how soon they pay out, and for what period of time. Most policies have a waiting period (ninety days is common for long-term, up to thirty days for short-term) before paying any benefits.

Short-term disability usually pays out for up to twenty-six weeks, while long-term commonly pays for up to five years, or age sixty-five, whichever comes first. Some policies will offer lifetime payouts, but come with costlier premiums.

Here are some things to look for when purchasing disability insurance:

- Purchase a noncancelable policy with guaranteed renewable coverage.
- Make sure that it includes "Own-Occupation" coverage, which pays if you're unable to work in your own occupation (even if you can do other work).
- You should have the longest benefit period you can afford (lifetime should cover you if you're permanently disabled).
- A COLA (cost-of-living-adjustment) provision will adjust your monthly payout for inflation.

When you're youngish, you can't imagine ever being disabled or even needing basic medical insurance. Then you have an emergency room visit followed by a hospital stay, concluding with a bill for $10,000+. In hindsight, insurance payments would have been a good idea. If you're the sole support of a family, you definitely need disability insurance.

> **Disability Insurance**
>
> As with any insurance policy, which is a form of contract, it's buyer beware. You could be buying a perfectly good policy, but that doesn't mean it's good enough for you. Do your research, talk with different agents, and be sure you're clear on costs and benefits. The policy language will not read anything like the simpler, user-friendly text in the brochures or advertisements.

Medical

A commonly tossed-around figure states that almost 47 million Americans have no medical insurance. Medical bills are a common cause of personal bankruptcy filings, and no small amount of anxiety for those who can barely afford to pay as they go. I've had two on-the-job injuries that required medical attention. The last one needed six sutures and ran over $1,800 for a very brief procedure. This is cash out of your pocket—and your family's—if you're without insurance.

A handyman has plenty of opportunities for cuts, gouges, falls, and worse. Disability insurance will not pay your medical bills. *You need medical insurance!*

Use www.ehealthinsurance.com to start your search on costs and policy availability.

If you're currently covered under an employer's health-care plan which falls under COBRA (Consolidated Omnibus Budget Reconciliation Act) rules, you can apply for a COBRA extension, which is a continuation of this coverage, paid for by you for a period of up to eighteen months. It's not necessarily the cheapest way to go, but assures continuous coverage until you take out an individual or family policy. For more information, go to www.dol.gov/ebsa/faqs/faq_consumer_cobra.HTML.

Automobile Insurance

When you use a personal vehicle for business use, it affects your insurance rates.
Your insurer might suggest the addition of a business endorsement, or tell you that
you need commercial auto insurance. A distinction is made between general contractor and artisan use. An artisan is a subcontractor or specialty contractor, such as
plumbing, electrical, drywall, and so on. As a handyman, insurance carriers see you
in a twilight zone since you carry out many types of work, but you do it all yourself.
Some carriers will not extend an endorsement for business use if they view a vehicle
as being used by an artisan.

Generally, if only one vehicle is used for the business and you're the only driver
(no employee usage), personal auto insurance will do. It's always up to your carrier, so
be certain you're perfectly clear about how the vehicle will be used. You'll be exposed
to more potential liability driving to customers' homes (regular exposure to kids on
bikes, dogs, pedestrians, etc.), and you want to have sufficient coverage to pay for
damages.

General Liability

You have liability coverage on your car; now you need it on you! As a handyman, you
need insurance to cover claims against you for property loss or damage, as well as
any injuries that result from your completed work or your presence during a job. The
simple task of hanging a picture on a bedroom wall can turn into a nightmare if you
puncture a pipe that leaks through a plaster ceiling, then all over an Oriental rug in
the living room below, along with the oak flooring underneath it. Plumbers have

been known to start the occasional fire when soldering pipes with propane torches, fires they were unaware of because they smoldered inside a wall and thus went unnoticed until it was too late.

If you think about it, the possibilities are endless, depending on the range of work you do. You could drop a brick off a roof while rebuilding a chimney and that brick could land on your customer's car—or on the customer. Forget to close a gate and a prize poodle runs off; brush up against an antique desk and leave a scratch; even a client tripping over a pile of debris you hadn't quite cleaned up yet—all of these can become expensive problems, aside from the physical and emotional damage they can cause your customers.

The cost of liability insurance varies depending on the carrier and the degree of protection you want. Some would recommend a million dollars in coverage, which isn't as outlandish as it might sound when you consider the degree of injury one mishap could cause. Compare the cost of a million-dollar policy with those in the hundreds of thousands of dollars; it might not be enough difference to forgo a million dollars in coverage.

Business Insurance

For a primer on business insurance, go to www.entrepreneur.com/insurancecenter, a resource guide from the publication *Entrepreneur*.

Employees will affect your insurance costs because they increase your risks. This is something to keep in mind if you're planning on eventually expanding your business.

Umbrella Policy

An umbrella policy is a relatively inexpensive way of purchasing additional insurance whose coverage goes beyond the usual liability coverage limits. This coverage provides extra protection if you have a large loss that isn't completely covered by your underlying coverage (see your insurance agent for details).

All this insurance talk sounds kind of ominous, suggesting that this scary, litigation-happy world is just waiting to trap you. What are the chances you'll ever have a claim? Well, how many claims have you had with your car or home? In all likelihood, not too many. Insurance is something you have to have for your own protection. No one likes paying for it, but everyone is grateful to have it when it's needed. *Remember: All policies must be kept current and renewed yearly.*

Additional Insured

If you ever do work for a general contractor, you might be required to add the general contractor to your automobile insurance as "Additional Insured" for the duration of the job. General contractors do this to protect themselves in the event you cause injury or damage with your vehicle while working on their job. Adding another party to your policy is normally an additional cost, so factor this in when bidding these jobs.

A Bonding Experience

Even if your word is your bond, the law requires something more. Unless your state or local jurisdiction has some odd exception, you will need to be bonded in order to legally run your handyman business. This means purchasing a surety bond for an amount of money determined by the state, or depositing an equivalent amount of cash or a certificate of deposit with the state for as long as you stay in business (and then some; see below).

What's with this bond requirement? What does *surety* mean? Isn't insurance enough?

■ The bond protects your customers should you, for any reason, not complete a job; if this happens, the customer can go after your bond.

■ *Surety* refers to "certainty."

■ A surety bond indicates there is a bond issuer or an amount of money that will guarantee the value of the bond.

■ It is not an insurance policy.

A $4,000 bond, for example, means that if a customer has a legitimate complaint against you for unfinished work, up to $4,000 can be paid to the customer out of your bond. If you purchase your bond through a bonding agency (often your insurance company), they will pay the customer and then you will repay the agency. For claims over $4,000, the customer will have to seek separate legal action.

Each state sets a value for the bonds required by general contractors and specialty contractors. As of this writing, the state of Arizona, for example, requires a $1,000 bond for residential specialty contractors grossing under $100,000 a year, and a $4,250 bond if the gross is between $100,000 and $375,000. In California, a bond costs $12,500.

Bonding Agency vs. (Your) Cash

Coming up with a cash bond can be burdensome if not impossible for some new business owners. That's where bonding agencies come in. For a small fraction of the value of the bond, paid by you in the form of a premium, they will assume the role of the surety. Your premium cost depends on how financially sound and reliable the bonding agency concludes you are after they review your application and snoop around some.

One advantage of going through a bonding agency, besides the much-lower up-front costs, is that all-cash bonds are retained by your state for a period of time after you close your business. California, for instance, will hold on to your money for three years, and Arizona for two. Why? The state wants to be sure there are no claims against you after you've closed up and gone on to bigger and better things.

Your state licensing department can provide you with its bonding requirements. Talk with your insurance agency about rates and shop around for some comparison quotes. There is no shortage of bonding agencies advertising online as well. As with any purchase, read the small print and be sure you're comparing apples with apples when looking at different quotes.

Licensing Bureaus

If you want to skip Google to find your state department of licensing, let the SBA do the job for you. Go to www.sba.gov/hotlist/license.html for a list of licensing bureaus. Keep in mind that links change, but these should get you where you want to go.

Let Me See Your License and Registration, Please

Your state and local governments wish you great success in your new venture, and they also wish to share in this success. Thus, you must register (in most cases), largely so taxes can be collected. Fees vary from state to state and within the state, as each city and town has its own tax structure. The city of Cleveland, Ohio, charges $15 plus a $5 registration fee for a business license application, whereas the state of Utah charges $210 for a specialty contractor's license. It isn't realistic to cover all states (let alone all local requirements) in one book, so inquire online with the appropriate agencies (Department of Labor and Industries, the treasurer, tax department, city hall, etc.) for the necessary forms and fees. At the same time, you will be registering the legal name of your business.

What's in a Name?

You can register your business under your own name or under an assumed or fictitious name. Jane Doe Handy Services is the legal name of a sole proprietorship owned by Jane Doe. She might decide she would rather be doing business as (DBA) Hula Girl Home Repairs. Jane Doe must register the company under one name or the other. The fictitious DBA name can incur a minor additional fee depending on the state of registration. You must have your DBA registration if you wish to open a bank or credit account under that name.

For those for whom dealing with layers of government is a less than fun experience, leave it to other entrepreneurial types to come up with a solution. For a fee, you can simplify your applications by using businesses whose mission is to help you get licensed. Two that show up prominently on the Internet are www.businesslicenses .com and www.businessnameusa.com. Both offer license forms and filing services. If they get you through the process faster, they might be worth the extra cost. In any event, they're certainly worth exploring.

Legal Eagles and Number Crunchers

You're just getting started—do you really need a lawyer and an accountant, both of whom will be charging more per hour than you'll ever charge? As usual, it depends.

Some would argue that the time to have an attorney, or at least to have one lined up, is when you *don't* need an attorney—that is, when you have no pressing legal needs and want to avoid any legal problems. Fair enough.

Standard Start-Up Costs Summary

SALARIES

Owner's

Employee(s)'

INSURANCE

Liability

Auto

Medical

Disability

BOND REGISTRATIONS

State

Local

VEHICLE

Truck, car, or van

New or used

MARKETING

Paid-for advertising

Business cards, brochures, Internet

Free giveaways

ATTORNEY

ACCOUNTANT

MATERIALS

Office-related

Supplies for jobs

Look for a lawyer who understands small businesses and perhaps whose practice is also a small business. You want someone you're comfortable with, who is affordable, and will keep you out of trouble.

Attorneys are useful if you're being sued or if you have to chase someone for a substantial amount of money due. Your general liability should be covered by your insurance.

Your books and accounts, at this point, will be very, very simple, nothing you can't handle. The tax forms for a sole proprietorship are not complicated; you list your expenses, any big-ticket items you might be depreciating (more on this later), and whatever money you have left over after deducting all these costs from your yearly income.

Forming a partnership? Consider a lawyer unless you want to study up on the necessary requirements; same with incorporating. This book cannot serve as a definitive legal or tax guide; it can only provide the most likely scenarios for your new small business. Anything can happen, even catastrophic events, causing you to curse yourself (and me) for not having had legal or accounting advice prior to those events, but they're not likely to occur. Hiring these professionals at any point in your business career will simply depend on how complex your business has become, or your degree of comfort dealing with your legal and financial affairs on your own. If you do decide on consulting with either an accountant or an attorney at the start of your business, get an estimate up front for the cost of your sessions. For more on taxes, see chapter 8.

Smaller-Ticket Items

We've discussed the big items you'll have to calculate in to both your start-up costs and your first year's expenses. Now it's time for everything else. You will become acutely aware, as you get further along in your new business, that everything is costing you money: the gas for your car, the trips to the paint store, your updated software, new tools. It all adds up, and until you begin collecting fees for your work, you will have to have the capital to cover these expenses.

Materials

You'll need some basic materials—sandpaper, caulk, small plumbing and electrical parts, paintbrushes, roofing tar—to cover miscellaneous jobs. You want to have as many materials and tools as you can comfortably carry so that you're prepared to do other jobs for a customer in addition to the specific ones you were called to do. This way, you won't miss out on an opportunity to increase your revenue and show your versatility.

Purchasing these materials represents:

- an investment of your time and money;
- a benefit to your customer, who did not have to go out and purchase anything or spend time doing so; and
- a possible profit center.

Some contractors advertise that they do not mark up their materials, providing the receipts to their customers. Others keep the receipts and mark everything up at least 10 percent or more, and do not list the materials as a separate item on their invoices. Without any markup, you will either have to charge a higher hourly amount or bill directly for the time you spend picking up the materials. Either is a viable strategy. However, the one drawback to listing the materials separately is your customer might find your cost excessive because you didn't choose a less-expensive supplier, or you didn't purchase an item during a recent sale. Consider both approaches during this financial planning stage of your business and then stick with one. Normally, you're better off not itemizing the materials and simply charging by the job, although some billings will reflect a partial materials list, as in, "Installed one NuTone QT exhaust fan."

Marketing

You might find yourself so busy from the get-go that the last thing you need to do is any marketing. Short of that, you'll have to get the word out. The sky's the limit when it comes to how much you can spend, but that doesn't mean all the money will be well spent.

The old standby has been the Yellow Pages, a hard-copy phone book. If you're of a certain age, this seems viable; if you're of another certain age, you never use a phone book for anything other than a doorstop. For the price of a Yellow Pages ad—a price you will be paying monthly until your contract is up—you can produce an awful lot of flyers, brochures, and business cards. One advantage: If your local edition has a handyman category, you will have way fewer competitors listed than, say, dentists or dog groomers.

Some marketing won't cost you anything but your time and a few sheets of paper as you go around and introduce yourself to real estate agents, small business owners, and property managers. A well-designed and executed sign on your vehicle—you could even attach a magnetic, weatherproof plastic business card holder near the sign so potential customers can get your card when you're parked near a job—will grab plenty of attention. Be willing to pay a local artist or sign company whatever it takes for a sign that gets you noticed.

To establish your marketing budget:

- Inquire about ad rates for the Yellow Pages and local newspapers.
- Price business cards, flyers, and brochures with volume discounts.
- Get quotes on a sign for your vehicle, either detachable, window-mount, or directly painted.

Marketing Tips

We all like free stuff, whether we need it or not. If there's a community fair coming up, consider ordering some balloons with your company name and phone number printed on them. Get a few tanks of helium, put on your company T-shirt, and give the balloons away to kids. It's a great opportunity to talk with their parents. Do an Internet search for business promotional materials and evaluate the pens, candies, and other giveaway items that can also carry your printed name.

Regardless of what you spend on advertising, your return will be limited to a modest percentage of the people who read your ads or accept your flyers. Getting yourself out personally in the public's eye and meeting the neighbors of your customers will always get you more business. I've seen it time and time again. One painter I knew got all of his business that way; I don't think he *ever* advertised. Every time he painted the exterior of a house, he ended up bidding two or three others in the neighborhood. The exterior work would then lead to interior work in the fall and winter months.

Make Marketing Personal

Yellow Pages advocates are very fond of this familiar, basically universal book distributed throughout the country. In one recent study for the Yellow Pages Association, it was claimed that 87 percent of the U.S. population used the paper version of the Yellow Pages in 2007. Almost 25 percent of the population is under eighteen years of age (do you know anyone that young using the Yellow Pages?), and an estimated 8 percent of U.S. households have no landlines, suggesting cell phones (or no phones) only. Eliminate the very elderly, those in extended-care facilities, the severely disabled, and so on, and the 87 percent figure is debatable. Do your own research before investing in these expensive ads. Here's one starting point: http://ezinearticles.com/?Yellow-Pages-Advertising-Tips---The-Straight-Facts-About-Yellow-Pages-Usage&id=964442.

Taxes

Depending on your state and local departments of revenue, you will most likely have some tax liability in the form of business taxes based on your revenues. They will not be monumental, but should be accounted for in your overhead. If you have employees, you must pay:

- 7.65 percent of their FICA or Social Security and Medicare contributions; and
- unemployment taxes, both state and federal (SUTA and FUTA).

Since no one is paying your FICA contributions, those are left up to you as well, and they're not cheap. To quote the IRS (www.irs.gov/businesses/small/article/0,,id=98846,00.html):

> *SE tax rate. The self-employment tax rate is 15.3%. The rate consists of two parts: 12.4% for social security (old-age, survivors, and disability insurance) and 2.9% for Medicare (hospital insurance).*
>
> *Maximum earnings subject to SE tax. Only the first $102,000 of your combined wages, tips, and net earnings in 2008 is subject to any combination of the 12.4% social security part of SE tax, social security tax, or railroad retirement (tier 1) tax.*
>
> *Computing FUTA tax. For 2008 and 2009, the FUTA tax rate is 6.2%. The tax applies to the first $7,000 that you pay to each employee as wages during the year. The $7,000 is the federal wage base. Your state wage base may be different. Generally, you can take a credit against your FUTA tax for amounts that you paid into state unemployment funds. This credit cannot be more than 5.4% of taxable wages. If you are entitled to the maximum 5.4% credit, the FUTA tax rate after the credit is 0.8%.*

For more on taxes, please see chapter 8.

Enough with These Expenses; Let's Talk Income

In your past life, you probably worked for wages: so many hours of your time for either so much an hour or a lump sum every two weeks. It was all very predictable. If you were hourly, the only opportunity you had for more money was overtime. Periodic pay increases would try and keep up with the increase in cost of living.

Now, as you're about to go out on your own, you have more opportunities for a higher income because you can set your rates and your hours. If you can manage it, you can work a hundred hours a week (until you collapse, anyway). You will also be paying for everything needed to earn this income, and absorbing any losses from downtime or errors in your bids. It's pretty self-evident that you want to minimize your losses and maximize your income.

At this point, you have to nail down your fees, including any minimum fees for showing up or for doing particularly challenging jobs.

Hourly or by the Job?

Many jobs can be done for a set rate. Mechanics, for example, refer to a flat-rate book when estimating some repairs (so much to replace brake pads, for instance). You'll develop your own flat rates using nationally publicized figures or your own experience for jobs that are pretty definable and for the most part will not present much variance. Yes, there's always the chance of some variance, and that's why you make it clear that your estimate or rate is based on not running into any problems. Replacing a wall light switch in a modern house is very straightforward, whereas old knob-and-tube wiring can require adding pigtails (short wires) if the existing wire ends are corroded and need to be snipped off. Even so, you can always establish a separate price for dealing with knob-and-tube wiring.

Flat-rate jobs can be very profitable when you can finish them sooner than expected. You have to establish a rate that will cover you for most conditions on specific jobs without making the rate so high that your potential customer calls someone else.

Some jobs don't lend themselves to flat rates, such as cleaning gutters. Until you see the job and how easy or difficult the gutters are to access, you can't give an exact price over the phone. You can state a price range that gutter cleaning normally falls under—say, $150 to $200 for most 1,500-square-foot, two-story homes—if this has been your experience. The same is true for some painting and carpentry repairs; you have to see the job before you can figure out how long the work will take you and how much the materials will cost. You could provide a customer with a cost, for instance, of so much a lineal foot to install baseboards, but if your customer doesn't have the footage or the inclination to measure, you can't come up with a final figure without looking at the job.

The same is true if someone asks you to repair a deck, sight unseen. You can offer all the costs-per-foot quotes you want, but until you see the deck, you don't know how much repair is needed. You have to decide if it's worth the time to give an on-site estimate or risk losing the job.

Another approach is time and materials only, plus profit and overhead. You might not make the easy profits on fast jobs, but you won't take any losses due to underestimating. Most customers will want a more definitive price and estimate, however.

What Should You Charge?

You can charge whatever you like; whether you get it or not is another story. Your rates should be competitive for where you live and for your level of competence.

To determine your hourly rate, you can Google "salary calculator" and get an idea of the yearly income for carpenters, painters, and related trades, but these calculators don't factor in that you're self-employed. Craigslist.com lists individuals offering "skilled trades," few of whom are licensed, and whose rates are either listed or available through e-mail. Another site, www.costhelper.com, lists researched costs for various home-repair jobs, as well as other consumer items and services.

Although it's not an entirely fair use of their time, by calling local handymen, both independents and franchise operators, you can get prices for whatever jobs you inquire about, as well as their basic hourly rate. You might also try your local chamber of commerce, as they might have information on local fees for a variety of businesses and services.

Once you establish your hourly rate:

- decide on a minimum fee for any job (in other words, for showing up);
- calculate a travel charge (optional, as this can be included in overhead); and
- stick to your rates.

This is exactly what appliance repair shops do, only in their business, they can only offer a limited diagnosis over the phone as to what repairs they will actually need to do. When a customer says the dishwasher has stopped running, the problem could be anything from a tripped circuit breaker to a burned-out motor. The customer pays regardless of what work is done, or, if the estimated work is declined, pays a service charge for hearing the bad news.

Negotiating Fees

You can always negotiate your rates and fees without unduly compromising your-self. Why would you? You might need the work, or a customer might have enough additional work to do that it's worth offering a deal, since you're already on the job and set up. Also, consider discounts if you think it will help your business. Senior discounts are common, but you can define your discount group as you wish (single parents, religious institutions, or your child's softball team).

Your job rates and your hourly rate should figure in your overhead, which includes the time spent:

- giving estimates;

- writing up bills;

- chasing down supplies;

- dealing with bad debts—someone who doesn't pay or writes a bad check; and

- returning to a completed job to correct a problem (callback).

There was one painter in Seattle some years back who charged for his estimates, so I thought, why not? They were very time-consuming, and it was fairer to bill those for whom he was estimating (and who might not give him the work) than passing on the fees in his overhead to those customers who hired him. Another part of his policy was to refund the estimate fee if his bid was accepted. Given the size of most handyman jobs, charging for estimates is unrealistic, but I still like the idea.

Is It Enough?

As the dollar signs float in front of your eyes, now is the time for another reality check: Will you earn enough from your handyman business to maintain or obtain the life-style you want? Can you earn enough each week to pay the bills, save, and invest? You should assume some downtime as well. While you had Thanksgiving off with pay when you worked for someone else, no one will be paying you now. Fewer people will want you mucking around their house during the holiday season, unless something absolutely has to be done, so you can end up with even more unpaid time.

Some jobs will bring in less money than you expect if your estimate is off. If you get sick or injured, that lost income stays lost. This is reality, and you have to factor it in. On the positive side, if you're making enough money, you'll welcome the freedom of taking time off when you wish. This is a big plus to self-employment.

Savings Through Deductions

Keep in mind that some of your overhead—vehicle and office expenses, for instance—is tax-deductible, and you'll incur some savings with these deductions.

If the Numbers Don't Work Out . . .

You really want to be a handyman and give up your current job, slogging away at a computer in your engineering job. You've added up all your expenses, looked at your budget, and estimated how much you need to earn to make all this happen.

And it isn't happening. Then you should:

- Stop and take a breath.
- Don't panic; this can probably still work out.
- Refigure.
- Go over all your figures again, checking for accuracy, and try them again.
- Reconsider.
- Calculate what you will have to change (cut your expenses, increase your rates, or plan on working more hours) to make this work.
- Consider whether you should put this business idea on the back burner for a while.

You're here and you've made it over some big hurdles: envisioning what you want to do, writing a business plan, and figuring out the money issues. Now you have to connect the dots and get your business up and running. There's paperwork to do, and fortunately, a lot of it can be done online (which should eventually force the retirement of the term paperwork). Internet searches will get you started with your business registration, insurance quotes, bank account fees, and even a business vehicle. A few fruitful hours with your computer and you can be pretty far along as a legal handyman.

Although we've already covered some of these steps, we'll touch on them briefly here.

One great way to get a good start on your business tax education is to get a copy of Internal Revenue Service Publication 583, *Starting a Business and Keeping Records* (www.irs.gov/pub/irs-pdf/p583.pdf). This twenty-seven-page guide is a wonderful source of information for anyone starting a new business, and includes all the basic federal tax information, a sample recordkeeping system, and sample forms.

Start-up Prep Work

Your start-up process won't happen overnight. It will take days (if not weeks) to get your insurance and bond in order and your various licenses processed. Keep this in mind if you're planning on leaving a current job. You'll be better off postponing your last day for a few weeks and maintaining your present income for as long as you can while you get everything in order.

First Things First

Since you normally have to show proof of insurance and a bond in order to get a license (check with your state licensing board), you will need to purchase your insurance policy and bond first. The most logical insurer to start with is the company currently insuring your home and/or automobile. They might not offer small business insurance, but they can certainly point you in the right direction by recommending an agency that does.

The Internet offers any number of insurance providers and immediate rate comparisons. (Warning: Read the fine print and confirm that the policies you're comparing will offer you the same level of protection.) You need to discuss your business needs with an agent who is knowledgeable about small businesses, especially those in the construction and home-repair trades. Remember: The lowest price isn't necessarily the best price. You want an insurer that's reliable and pays off claims in good time without reenacting the Spanish Inquisition.

Finding an Insurance Provider

Check your prospective business insurer with the National Association of Insurance Commissioners (www.naic.org). You'll want to know if they have a sound history or one that's filled with complaints. Also, be sure to Google "consumer reviews" on any company you're considering for your insurance.

Other good sources for insurer recommendations are small contractors who are already doing similar work, including painters, landscapers, plumbers, and so on. Before talking with any agent, prepare a profile of yourself and your business (if you've done your business plan, you can cut and paste the pertinent text into a new document) and the type of work you'll be doing. This saves a lot of back-and-forth with the agent and allows a better risk assessment in order to come up with the best policy for you. Since there's a chance you'll be doing some commercial work, be sure your policy covers construction sites as well. If not, you might be charged a small additional premium as these jobs occur on a case-by-case basis.

The Name Is Bond . . . Surety Bond

Next up is your bond. An all-cash bond, whose price is determined by your state's requirements per contractor classification, is the most expensive way to go up front. In the long run, it can be less expensive than paying a bonding agency year after year, but if you need the cash for other start-up costs, consider using an agency at this time.

Start with your insurance company, as most large property and casualty companies also issue surety bonds. The surety agency will do a prequalifying check on you and your financial background to assure themselves you're a reasonable risk. Any surety agency operating in your state is licensed by the state department of insurance. You can confirm that your chosen agency is approved by going to the National Association of Insurance Commissioners site, www.naic.org/state_web_map.htm.

For more information on surety companies, go to The Surety & Fidelity Association of America's Web site, www.surety.org.

Licensing

You normally need a state license and most likely a local one for your municipality. Requirements regarding counties, or their equivalent, vary from state to state. Ultimately, every government department that wants to know about you and collect taxes from you will require that you register with them. If you're uncertain as to the total requirements, your municipality will cheerfully inform you.

Your state licensing process will also register you with the Department of Labor and Industries if you have (or plan on having) any employees. And just what do these departments do?

- They collect workers' compensation and unemployment taxes.
- Workers' compensation provides cash payments to workers injured on the job.
- Unemployment taxes provide state unemployment insurance payments to qualifying workers who have lost their jobs.

How long will the licensing process take? According to www.businessnameusa .com, a business licensing firm, "In most states, regular registration filing takes 4–8 business days, but in some states it may take 10–20 business days because the government processing takes longer. Where it is permitted by the government, there is same-day filing for an extra fee."

Is Your Name, *Your* Name?

Before applying for your license, be sure the name you've chosen for your business is available. Check with your secretary of state's office and look for a name-search feature (e.g., www.tennesseeanytime.org/sosname/ for the state of Tennessee). Otherwise, your application will be delayed and you'll have to come up with another catchy moniker.

If you plan on having employees from the start, you will need an Employer Identification Number (EIN), available at www.irs.gov or from your local IRS office.

Banking

If you're really disciplined and don't use your checking account for much, you could get along by using your personal account to pay for your business expenses. Just put a star or asterisk at every entry that's business-related and tally up later. But what are the chances of that happening? Easier yet, just open a separate account, which makes your bookkeeping simpler and the IRS happier should you ever go through an audit.

You can research the best deal on a checking account online, which beats doing it over the telephone or on foot. Even your small-town banks will have Web sites listing their checking account options. It's tempting to buy a BIG check register with multiple checks per page, but think about it. Most of your purchases will be on account or with a credit or debit card. If you use online payments, you'll rarely write any checks. My preference is a standard single-check-display checkbook, the same kind you'd use for personal purposes. Let's face it: Checks are old technology, although they do offer the advantage of a few days' float when paying your bills—meaning the money stays in your account until the check you've written clears. A few large contractors I once dealt with wrote payment checks using an out-of-state bank to increase the float. This made sense for them, given that they were writing millions of dollars' worth of checks a year, but as the recipient, I didn't appreciate it.

Balancing Act

It sounds obvious, but keep your checkbook balanced as you use it, and always balance it against your monthly bank statement! Although their error rate is quite low, banks are not error-free. You must scrutinize your statements for accuracy, and if you find any discrepancies:

- review the previous month's statement to be sure any differences were accounted for;
- ensure that all outstanding checks are listed;
- check your subtraction and addition;
- be sure you wrote the correct check and deposit amounts in your register; and
- account for all bank charges that weren't part of your running balance.

Consider a dedicated credit card for your business as well, *and pay the bill off every month!* The amount of consumer installment credit so many Americans are buried under is bad enough; you don't want to be paying off business expenses the same way. Keep your billing in order and up-to-date, and your collections, too. Pay off your vendor bills with the income from the jobs that incurred those bills. Do you really want to spend a year or two paying off paint or fencing material or roofing tar because you're stretching your payments out? It's a bad idea, so don't even start. Pay as you go and you'll be much better off. (Not that I have an opinion about it or anything.)

The Tax Collector Cometh

Expect to pay your federal, state, and local taxes every three months. The state and your municipality will send you quarterly reporting forms after you've registered your business. Even if you have no income for the three-month period, you will still need to file the forms. Every state has different forms and taxes, but you can expect to pay:

- state withholding and unemployment taxes if you have employees;
- sales taxes (collected from customers if your services and products are subject to sales tax);
- any other state taxes levied on business owners (e.g., transit taxes); and
- local municipality business and occupation taxes and sales taxes.

The last item can only be defined as taxes due because of the fact that you're running a business. They vary by rate and by name (in Washington State, for instance, they're called Business and Occupation [B&O] taxes, while in New York City, if you're an unincorporated business, you pay an Unincorporated Business Tax [UBT]). See chapter 8 for more information on taxes.

To procure the federal tax forms you'll need, both for yourself and for any employee withholding, go to www.irs.gov/businesses/small/index.html. As a sole proprietor, either with or without employees, you will need:

- *Schedule C, Profit or Loss from Business* for your yearly tax return (combined with your 1040); and
- *1040-ES Estimated Tax* for your quarterly income tax payments.

If you have employees, you can add the following to your pile of required tax forms:

- *W-2* and *W-3* forms for withholding federal income taxes, Medicare, and Social Security contributions;
- *Form W-4* for your employee(s) to fill out;
- *Form 941, Employer's Quarterly Federal Tax Return*; and
- *Form 8109, Federal Tax Deposit Coupon* (it goes along with Form 941).

Starting to get confused? Who wouldn't; these are tax forms. For a good overall explanation, go to the IRS site and look at Publication 4591, *Small Business Federal Tax Responsibilities.*

Dreaming of a Paperless Office

The paperless office was going to be a reality in the 1980s—no, the 1990s—wait, not quite yet . . . more like the early twenty-first century. . . . It isn't here yet, so you're still stuck with paper for your billings and contracts, except for your hipper customers who prefer everything electronically delivered. That's all right; there are unlimited sources of printing companies and office supply stores that will satisfy your every paper need.

Or you can print many of your own.

You can complicate your accounting and billing as much as you want, or keep it simple. For those who prefer paper and ink, any office supply store will have accounting ledgers available. These are books with multicolumn pages to fill in according to your chosen expense and payment categories (supplies, taxes, bank deposits, and so on). For that matter, you could also use the BIG check register I mentioned, but didn't recommend, earlier for keeping your accounts. I still don't recommend it. Get a separate accounting book—Dome Publishing (www.domeproductsonline.com/) has several, and they do a good job.

For you paperphobes, accounting software is the way to go, including:

- Intuit's QuickBooks (http://quickbooks.intuit.com/)
- Microsoft Small Office Accounting (www.microsoft.com/smallbusiness/products/Financial-Management.aspx)
- Peachtree Complete Accounting Software (www.peachtree.com/peachtree accountingline/)

To varying degrees, accounting software allows you to integrate many tasks online: your bookkeeping, accounting, and banking; writing checks; and printing out billing and invoice forms.

What about general database information? After all, you have customer information, pricing, product lines, supplies, and calendar-based functions to deal with—that's a lot to keep straight using paper notebooks. Intuit offers very reasonably priced Web-based applications for business in their QuickBase product line. You can even design your own program using a series of templates—no programming knowledge required! Go to http://quickbase.intuit.com/home/video/ for more information.

On-site Electronics

Want to stay all-electronic on the road? Instead of using preprinted invoices, buy a mobile printer. Combined with a laptop PC, you can type out every invoice at the completion of the job using an invoice template and print it out immediately for your customer. This way, you won't have to do any data entry later on when it comes to invoices and accounting. All major printer companies have mobile printers available.

An online search for free accounting software brings up a number of freeware programs for those on a tight budget. Like any freeware, the programs will have limitations, and it could be troublesome to move any stored data from one of these programs to an off-the-shelf proprietary program later should you decide to purchase one.

Personalizing Invoices

You can create your own invoice using Microsoft Word or other word processing program. They don't have to be fancy. Set it up on your letterhead with the date, the heading invoice, the customer's name and contact information, the work performed, and the fee charged—or use one of Word's invoice forms. You won't need more than a few a day, so they can be economically printed on your own office printer.

Estimates and Contracts

You should establish your fees for standard jobs—door replacement, faucet repair, and so on—early on in order to you provide telephone and e-mail quotes. Given that many of your jobs will be under a thousand dollars, you can't afford to be driving around giving estimates, although if a customer's neighbor stops by while you're working and asks you to take a look at a job, by all means, do so. Before you start a new job, provide the customer with a written agreement so there will be fewer misunderstandings about the scope of work or your anticipated costs. Contracts are subject to interpretation, so the key is to be as clear as possible in all your spoken and written communications.

Your jobs will be relatively simple and limited in scope. For legal protection, contractors often use somewhat ominous-sounding estimate, bidding, and contract forms, and this isn't a bad idea. The standard information in these forms includes:

- your business name and contact information;
- customer's name and address;
- description of the work ("We propose to provide all the labor and materials to do the following . . .");
- proposed fee and how it is to be paid;
- time period for which the bid is valid (two weeks, thirty days, etc.); and
- standard boilerplate clause indicating all work will be done in a workman-like manner according to standard industry practices; anything beyond the described work is extra; the contractor is fully insured; and any disputes arising from the transaction will be settled in a court of law or by arbitration.

Estimating Unusual Jobs

What about jobs that don't have standard descriptions or fit exactly within unit costs? You write up a contract with all the known information and estimated allowances for the unknowns, or requested substitutions (e.g., customer requests additional coats of finish beyond a standard number). Adjust your estimate to include overhead and profit, and have the customer sign off. If it simply isn't feasible to arrive at a precise estimate or allowance, give it your best effort and consider billing for time and materials plus overhead and profit.

This seems like a lot for cleaning some windows or repairing a deck railing, but when thousands or tens of thousands of dollars are on the line, these contracts are critical. You could print up a reduced version of the one below on a postcard-size document and still be adequately covered for small jobs.

Print two of these to a page on cardstock, cut in half with a guillotine-style paper cutter, get a signature on both, and you have an easy-to-file record and a somewhat unique contract form for your customers. Or just use standard 8.5-by-11-inch paper, which is easier yet, and print two full-sheet copies. You can use your own word processing template or a purchased form available with business software packages.

The advantage of preprinted forms is that they can be ordered with carbon copies, but you'll end up either handwriting out all the descriptive information or typing it in—and who owns a typewriter these days? You can also use dynamic forms online. Some businesses offer contractors' forms that allow you unlimited use for a fee. You type the pertinent information inside the fields and print the completed form, but you can do the same thing with a word processing template, so there's little advantage to these services.

Until you get involved with larger, more complicated jobs, you should not require any lengthy contract forms.

Come Prepared

Always carry catalogs and product books for hardware, lighting, locksets, etc., to show customers should they express an interest in additional work. Also present them when bidding new work.

Harpo's Handyman Repair Service

123 Oak Street

Baltimore, MD

DATE: _____

JOB: B. Santos

160 Wild Apple Ave.

Baltimore, MD

WE PROPOSE TO: Refinish double entry doors, exterior side only. Existing doors will be stripped, sanded as needed, stained as per client's color choice, and coated with three applications of exterior high gloss polyurethane. Brass kick plates will be buffed, polished, and clear-coated. Surrounding work area will be protected with drop cloths. Job should take three days (one day per coat drying time). Doors must be kept open each day until dry to avoid damaging the finish. This bid is good for two weeks from today's date.

FEES AND TERMS: $950 plus sales tax of 5.75% for total of $1,009.63 payable upon completion

All work will be performed in a workmanlike manner according to standard industry practices. Requested work beyond proposal is an extra cost when approved by the client. Agreement contingent on delays beyond our control (e.g., weather). If any legal action occurs as a result of this agreement, the prevailing party shall be entitled to recover legal fees and reasonable costs of litigation as determined by a court of law.

ACCEPTED BY: _____   DATE _____

Bidding

Bidding a job will first introduce you to the client, for whom you must get a "feel," and the worksite and expected work conditions. Both will affect your pricing and whether you will even accept the job.

Bidding by Telephone or E-Mail

- Saves travel time

- Works for common jobs, such as replacing a ceiling light

- Must be clear with client that the bid price is an estimate only; the fee can change depending on the actual job conditions

- If bidding by e-mail, client can send photos to help clarify detail

On-Site Bidding

- More accurate, but time-consuming

- Must be scheduled in, often done in the evening or over a weekend

- Bid should allow for unseen conditions

- Not practical for smaller jobs; should be reserved for larger, more complicated work

Watch Out for Customer . . .

- Trying to find out from you how to do the job so they can do it themselves

- Appears too demanding or particular—the job results might never satisfy them

- Telling you multiple bids are being solicited for a modest-size job

- Who is extremely talkative and will be home while the work is being done

Bidding should allow for the following:

- An occupied home vs. a vacant one

- The presence of pets and children

cont.

cont.

- Accessibility

- Weather

- Travel time within the house (e.g., moving materials up and down the stairs or out to garage work area)

- Degree of clean-up required

- Difficulty in obtaining materials

- Unusual time requirements / emergency situation

Confirm your appointment to bid the day before. Refrain from doing so before entering the client's home. Offer to remove your shoes or bring along disposable shoe covers. Propose a range of options, if possible, and a realistic time frame to do the job. Be clear about any resulting dust and noise while working. Contact the clients in two or three days if you haven't heard from them regarding your bid.

Marketing Materials

Before the age of personal computers and printers, a business owner was at the mercy of print shops and designers for any and all marketing materials. Not any longer. With common software programs and free or inexpensive artwork, you can produce all (or most) of your promotional materials right in your own office. For large quantities of printing, it's not economical to use an office printer, but for short runs or samples, you can't beat them.

If you already have a graphics program such as Adobe's InDesign, then you're well positioned to create your marketing materials. There's no reason, however, to spend hundreds of dollars on graphics software when word processing programs are more than adequate. You're pitching handyman services, not interior design. As with accounting software, there are free word processing programs available online, offered with the usual caveats regarding their limitations and perhaps limited technical support, for those with challenged software budgets. For one example, look at Google Docs (http://docs.google.com/templates), which offers online storage and multiple user access.

For more information on marketing materials, please see chapter 10.

Graphic Artistes

Do you think of yourself as all thumbs when it comes to creative design? Feel compelled to hire a graphic artist to create a logo or brochures for you? Remember who you are: You're a handyman. No one is expecting, nor desiring, beautiful marketing materials, but everyone is expecting good repair work. Graphic artists are great for a lot of things but they're overkill for your needs. There are plenty of templates available for very presentable marketing materials. If you want some knockout photographs, go to a site such as www.istockphoto.com and purchase some to dress up your brochures and flyers.

You won't need a lot of paper-based promotional materials to get started, but you'll need some:

Business cards

Basic informational flyers and brochures

Business Cards

A business card can display as much or as little information as you want. Most are very basic, with name and contact information and a company logo, but a business card can be so much more.

A business card has two sides—use both of them.

- The reverse can be a list of all your services, for example, or a discount coupon ("Present this card for a 10 percent discount on your next service call.").
- Include information on stain removal or an abbreviated yearly maintenance schedule ("Spring: general cleaning, remove storm windows, check for damaged roof shingles, till garden space; Summer: paint exterior, etc.").
- You can even list interesting or unusual local attractions and their phone numbers—anything to help ensure that your card is looked at more than once and saved.

The more elaborate the card—glossy finishes, multiple colors, raised letters—the more expensive the printing costs. If you're trying to keep your costs down, go for a basic card, but add as much information and visual appeal as you can. Do an online search for "business card design" for some interesting ideas.

Order at least five hundred cards—better yet, order a thousand and give them out everywhere and to everyone.

Business Cards and More . . . for Cheap

Costco offers printing services in their stores with business centers. Their prices are very competitive, with quick turnaround times. Plus, you can buy some business-related supplies (cleaners, for instance) and cheap lunches (at those locations with cafés) as well.

Flyers and Brochures

Once again, your word processing program—or Microsoft Publisher, if you have their office suite—comes through with flying colors when it comes to producing brochures and flyers. Easy-to-use templates—you choose from a decent variety—allow you to fill the pages with brilliant prose about you and your company. You can even send the file electronically to a print shop and have them do the rest (be sure to talk with them first about formatting). Flyers and brochures give you plenty of space to list your services, fee structure, contact information, and occupational background.

Make your design stand out! Otherwise, your marketing material will get tossed away before it's read (many *will* be tossed out regardless, but you want to minimize this). You don't have to be Michelangelo to produce an effective flyer. Do an online search on "how to design a flyer" or something similar and read some free ideas. Think back to flyers and brochures that caught your attention and incorporate the features you remember.

You don't want to saturate the paper with text; think bullet points and white space. Before you have anything printed:

- Reread and proof your text thoroughly.
- Have someone else do it as well—preferably someone whose work includes a healthy dose of writing or editing (it's natural to miss errors in our own writing).

- You want your written materials to be accurate, with correct spelling, punctuation, and grammar.

How many should you print? Brochures printed on two sides and in need of folding will cost more than single-sided flyers, so I would start with flyers. At pennies apiece, you can easily do a few thousand.

Leave Yourself Behind

Appliance and heating repair companies regularly leave self-adhesive foil labels stuck to furnaces, appliances, or inside cabinet doors. The labels have the company name and contact information printed on them for future reference. You can do the same and leave them in appropriate spots before leaving your jobs such as inside a cabinet door under a kitchen or bathroom sink or inside a telephone book (don't leave them where they will upset your clients, such as stuck to the front of a refrigerator door).

Finding Suppliers

As you turn your handyman skills into a business, you'll find new vendors for some of the supplies and materials you've previously purchased at home improvement stores and your neighborhood hardware store. Why? As a business, you'll be able to purchase products wholesale—that is, at a discounted price—and typically will not pay any sales tax. (Your customer pays the sales tax on any materials used on the job because the customer is the end user, and you are reselling the materials; when you purchase for the purpose of reselling, you do not pay the sales tax unless your state has some exceptions.)

You will take a certain delight in your newfound wholesale world, as paint stores, hardware wholesalers, and lumber yards offer you lower prices and, to some extent, preferred service as you will become a repeat customer. It's like being in a special club, which, whether we care to admit it or not, is often appealing. Discount policies vary depending on the volume you're buying; for example, you won't get the same deal on a gallon of paint as a regional paint contractor who buys thousands of gallons a year.

Investigate the suppliers you expect to use and start the paperwork for setting up accounts with them. Offer to pay for your initial purchases at the time of purchase to establish some good faith and credibility. When you are later billed for the charges you have on your account, pay promptly. Even when the business climate is better than it is at the time of this writing, cash flow is important to everyone.

Debit When You Can

Your supplier is giving you a discount, so try not to pay for your materials with a credit card as this costs the supplier a percentage of the purchase price. Instead, use a debit card, assuming there are no fees for the merchant, or check.

Business Vehicles

You'll need a dependable vehicle. It won't look too professional if you have to cancel a job because your '82 Nissan isn't running and you're not sure how soon you can fix it. Consider your vehicle choice carefully. New vehicles are expensive and depreciate quickly. Leasing can be a losing proposition if you end up owing more than the vehicle is worth at the end of the lease. A clean, used car or truck that will accommodate the types of jobs you want to do—meaning, it will haul the required tools and materials safely and dependably—is all you need. Now is not the time to obligate yourself to purchase or lease payments.

Your Vehicle and the Law

As a business owner, you can investigate ordering commercial license plates for your vehicle. Depending on your local parking laws, these often allow you to park in commercial parking spaces and perhaps loading zones without incurring a ticket. Some laws require that your vehicle have a painted sign (as opposed to a removable sign) identifying your business before issuing commercial plates. Keep in mind that some insurance issues involve signage on your business vehicle.

Start-Up Checklist

Insurance
- Liability
- Consider a million dollars in coverage
- Vehicle
- Personal policy probably won't cover this; confirm additional coverage for business-related driving
- Disability (optional, but recommended)

Surety Bond
- Cash deposit is most expensive option up front
- Bonding agency charges fee for putting up the bond

License
- State
- Local
- Register with your department of labor and industries if you have or expect to have employees

Banking
- Business checking account
- Business credit card
- Online banking setup

Tax Forms
- IRS 1040-ES (estimated tax payments)
- State and local tax forms should be sent to you
- If you have employees:
    - IRS W-2, W-3, W-4
    - IRS Form 941 and Form 8109
- Request an Employer Identification Number (EIN) from the IRS

Billing, Estimating, and Contract Forms
- Print your own or use preprinted forms

Marketing Materials
- Business cards, flyers, and brochures

Line up your suppliers
- Establish your accounts, start filling out the paperwork

Business vehicle
- Be sure your vehicle is reliable and fits your budget

As much as you enjoy repairing the world, you have to spend some time in an office dealing with the dreaded paperwork (even if it's increasingly electronic). Computers have greatly simplified recordkeeping and document creation, but they haven't eliminated paper altogether, or the need to store it. Your office will represent both worlds, electronic and hard copy, and also serve as your fixed communication center.

Your office can be as plush or as spartan as you wish. With a notebook computer and a cell phone, you barely need a fixed office space. You can get by with a bookshelf to house your printer and paper files. That said, many business owners want an office for a feeling of legitimacy, and simply for some dedicated private space for themselves, away from partners, children, dogs, and house chores.

Sharing your professional space with your family's personal computer or gathering space isn't the best idea, even if you're short on extra space. As a handyman, you can create a space just about anywhere and run power and phone lines to it, unless you're going wireless and running off a home network. Then you only need electricity and you're ready to go.

The main point is that your office suite should provide you with privacy, light, and comfort. If you're happy working out of the furnace room, then move into the furnace room. We are all territorial to some extent, and you need to establish your territory, even if you have a very liberal open-door policy.

Filling the Space

Furniture, even if you're a minimalist, will be first on your list. Unlike the castigated Wall Street execs of late who can't seem to live without $3,000 wastebaskets, you need functional furniture that you don't mind getting a little scruffy when you plop yourself down dressed in work clothes, with some of the day's debris still clinging to you.

Large desks can be cumbersome and excessive, unless it's your style to spread out a lot of papers, electronics, pens, coffee cups, and family photos in front of you. Do you really need all those drawers? It can be argued that the more space we have available to us, the more stuff we'll find to fill it. Consider starting out with less storage space and see if it leads to less stuff.

Outfitting Your Office

Why buy any office furniture at all? Go to your local www.craigslist.com listings, open up the "free" category, and search for office furniture or desks. There are always free desks, shelves, storage containers, filing cabinets, and office chairs available as long as you're willing to transport them. Some of this furniture was very expensive when new and still in great condition; it's just no longer needed.

Take a Seat

After a long day of physical labor, any time spent in your office should be as comfortable as possible. Splurging on a decent office chair isn't a luxury. You don't have to spend hundreds of dollars on an admittedly very cool Herman Miller Aeron ergonomic wonder—you won't be in the office *that* often—but you don't have to contend with a wooden stool missing one leg, either.

Used office chairs start for as little as $20, and new ones not much over $100. Quality and comfort varies, of course, so find something you like, and don't be too stingy about the price. Think of the chair as a tool that you'll keep and depend on for years to come.

Shelving and Storage

Shelves are easy for a handyman to build or assemble. You'll be storing computer printer paper, reference books, marketing materials, and the assorted stuff of life. As with your other office furniture, look for free or used shelving online through craigslist.com or other community exchange sites.

Filing cabinets are a matter of personal taste. Unless you need to lock up your paper files, you'll have plenty of room on bookshelves to store those files.

Lighting

A 2007 *British Medical Journal* article on medical myths reported that reading in dim light won't damage your eyes, but it will cause discomfort. This isn't necessarily a license to set up your office with candlelight, but to use sufficient comfortable lighting that won't cause glare on your PC monitor nor make reading difficult.

Show and Tell

Dry-erase whiteboards are useful if you have employees and are running multiple jobs. Look for these used or free online. New economy boards start at under $50.

Technology Rules . . . with Exceptions

Neil Postman, a well-known educator and social commentator, wrote his books out in longhand on legal pads. He was not a fan of electronic files, unlike his publishers. He could get away with pen and paper because, well, he was Neil Postman (and he had a typist who transcribed his scribbles). Regardless of your beliefs about technology and its drawbacks, unless you want to turn every one of your written communications into a handwriting or typing exercise, stick with a computer and a printer.

For the purposes of your handyman business, you do not need the latest and greatest PC or software. You could have Windows 95 and a really old version of Microsoft Office suite and do all your office functions very nicely if you were only distributing hard copies. If you're going electronic, you need to be more up-to-date, but you don't have to break the bank in doing so.

New computers—all right, new Windows and Linux-based computers, less so Apple—are cheaper than ever. Used systems complete with various software packages sell for a fraction of their original purchase prices. For a few hundred dollars, you can buy a computer, monitor, sometimes with Microsoft Office and a printer thrown in. You can't afford not to have a computer at these prices.

Reliability of used electronics is always an issue, so you might prefer purchasing from a vendor who only sells refurbished units with warranties.

Generally speaking, a desktop model will be more robust than a notebook and offers larger monitor options, but a notebook offers more portability. Hyper-speed and mega amounts of memory are not that critical for your purposes—you're not gaming, and probably not running large graphics programs—so don't be too concerned about either feature. Your computer will produce text-laden docs and store their files, not much more, other than your online activity.

Computer-free Business

Would you really rather avoid using a computer? So be it; you can survive nicely without one. A print shop can make up your business cards without an electronic file, although there will be a setup charge. Brochures and flyers can by typed and photocopied, and you can use preprinted billing and estimate forms with carbon/carbonless copies for your other paperwork. Nothing is forcing you to join the computer world, although it does simplify a lot of business procedures.

Office Printer

The volume of printing you expect to do is a good way to determine the quality and cost of the printer you'll need to buy. If you have four clients a day and print out two copies of each billing, and a few estimate sheets, you'll print a dozen copies a day. That's not going to stress any printer very much, but as your workload increases, or you decide to print your own flyers, a heavier-duty machine is in order. Like your computer, you don't need the fastest machine on the market, just a good working model that will push out clean copies.

The cheapest printer isn't necessarily the best bargain—not if the refill ink cartridges are ridiculously priced. Look for a good-quality inkjet model that comes with scanning, copying, and faxing capabilities and check the cost of its refill cartridges. Multifunctional printers (MFP) start at just over $100, up to the $300 range for a small business model. An Internet search on consumer reviews for the models you're interested in will give you some idea of how they perform in real life.

> **To Fax . . . or Not**
>
> Fax machines are used less often these days, for two reasons: (1) Documents can easily be sent via e-mail; and (2) electronic faxing, also done via e-mail for a fee, is more reliable than sending paper faxes. You can skip electronic faxing altogether by simply scanning a document, such as a receipt for materials, saving it in another format, and e-mailing it as an attachment. Buying a multifunction printer with fax capability is fine for the few times a paper fax comes in handy, but there's little point in buying a separate fax with a dedicated phone line.

Connecting to the Outside World

For years, the world got by with standard dial-up telephone service. Then the Internet came along, demanding more speed, and tossed dial-up into history's dustbin, along with rotary phones, black and white televisions, and disco. You have three readily available choices for phone and Internet access, although not all of them will be available in all areas:

- DSL (Digital Subscriber Line)
- Cable
- Satellite

All three are many times faster than dial-up and allow independent use of telephones. DSL and cable require wiring to your house, while satellite is wireless. There is no end to the available packages various communications providers are ready to sell you, so compare carefully. Some subscribers, for instance, use cell phones exclusively for their phone service, and cable or satellite for all their television and data connections. It all comes down to costs, service availability, and convenience. Regardless of what you do, plan on having a cell phone. You'll need one on the road to stay in contact with customers and suppliers.

Cell Phones

Albert Einstein said, "The hardest thing to understand in the world is the income tax." Clearly the good professor never had to evaluate competing cell-phone plans. Just assume you'll need a cell phone. Then, do an Internet search on "comparing cell-phone plans" and try and wade through the claims. Even if you hate cell phones and have refused to join the millions of users up to now, you will need to stay in contact with your customers in the event you're stalled in traffic or must otherwise reschedule. If it's any consolation, you can deduct all or some of the phone costs from your taxes.

Some Gadgets

President Obama was feeling BlackBerry withdrawal symptoms when told he would have to give up his electronic buddy. Super-encrypted software came to his rescue— not that hackers all over the globe won't still try and snoop out his e-mail address. PDAs (personal digital assistants) such as the BlackBerry and some sophisticated smartphones have become the gadget of the month for many people. Do you need one?

Well, it's a personal preference, and a convenience when it comes to ordering theater tickets, checking your e-mail while on the road, and generally messing around online when you're bored. Bluetooth protocols allow your PDA to sync up with your computer and keep the data on both devices current. That's all very swell, but it won't necessarily help you clean out drains or replace a piece of broken glass.

One electronic gadget you *can* use to your advantage is a compact digital camera. Why? So you can photograph your jobs and record the conditions when you arrived, the work you performed, and the results and cleanup. If a client ever has questions or comments about what was done, you'll have proof to back yourself up.

You won't need the finest model that will do everything but provide you with photogenic models. There are plenty of decent cameras in the under-$200 range that will suit your purposes. Here are some things to look for when you research different models:

- Consider the number of megapixels (generally, the more the better, but pixel size matters, too).
- Battery life is important (longer is better).
- Avoid features you barely understand and will never use.
- Be sure the camera is comfortable to hold and manipulate.

A camera isn't critical, but photos can save you some grief if you have a disagreeable customer who later questions your work.

Photo Finish

Budget a little tight for a digital camera? Buy a camera phone for your cell phone and transfer the photos to your computer. The photos should be adequate until you can purchase a digital camera.

Your Business Web Site

We live in an electronically connected world, and your business can be part of this world. You can build (or hire someone else to build) your own Web site, highlighting:

- the type of work you do;
- your contact information;
- photos of some of your jobs (even a photo of you);
- your musings on home repairs;

- comments from your customers; and
- links to other useful sites.

For the price of a few caffeinated beverages every month, you can have a hosted Web site extolling your handyman virtues running 24/7 on the Internet. You'll need a:

- hosting service to run your site;
- a domain name (www.hilliaryshomerepair.com, for example); and
- a designed Web site.

Hosting services such as Bluehost (www.bluehost.com) offer very inexpensive packages for hosting, domain name searches (you have to confirm that your chosen site name isn't already in use), and site design. You don't have to code anything, as the design packages for do-it-yourselfers are template-based—you just have to fill in the fields. If you prefer, the hosting service will build the site for you, or you can hire your own site developer—but this starts costing money that's better spent elsewhere. You're not relying on your site for a lot of retail traffic where the coolest site design can affect sales.

Take a look at sites you like and try and duplicate the style and design within the limits of the templates provided by your hosting service. A clean, uncluttered site, thoughtfully presented, will help potential local clients find you as they go searching online for a handyman service. Please see chapter 11 for more information on Internet usage.

Your Presence on the Web

Keep your Web site updated. For instance, you can advocate seasonal maintenance at different times of the year, or offer an Internet special ("10 percent off for all first-time customers who mention our Web site."). As you add new services or employees, mention them as well. In terms of "search engine optimization" or your Web site's ability to draw a lot of viewers by its use of key search words, just having "handyman" on your site should boost its traffic.

E-mail

E-mail is one of the best features of the Internet. You can send all types of correspondence, including billings, and instantly maintain copies of what was sent and when it was sent. One problem with e-mail: *not checking it daily!*

It's easy to lose track of e-mail, but even the most rudimentary programs offer you filing options, whereas programs such as Microsoft Outlook or Windows Mail go much further. Either way, keep a few e-mail rules in mind:

- Answer your e-mail promptly, the same as you would telephone calls.
- Carefully read over any correspondence before sending it out.
- Keep your messages to the point.
- Insert only critical attachments.
- Avoid frequent e-mails to everyone on your customer list (seasons' greetings and newsletters are fine).

Other Office Supplies

You'll need some paper and paper-related items. Any office supply store will have the usual pens, paper, envelopes, paper clips, file storage units, and so on. Costco also sells printer paper at a good price. One case of economy white paper will last you for a long time.

Software

For some software aficionados, Microsoft will always be evil. They will forever bemoan the loss of competing products and will promote Linux or even freeware instead. I will not argue the technological fine points of their beliefs because I have no qualifications to do so. Microsoft won, they sell the most widely used software programs in the universe, and unless you want to spend your spare time on Linux discussion boards, stick with some mainstream software. Microsoft Office Suite includes word processing, spreadsheets, publishing, and e-mail management programs for around $170.

Look at it this way: You're a handyman; you know how to make do when you have budget constraints. If you need to save money until you're up and running, use the programs you have. Every Windows operating system comes with Notepad, a more rudimentary word processing program, but more than sufficient for basic docs. Microsoft Paint, which also comes with Windows, allows you some room to create

artwork for your documents. (Paint is very versatile; take a look at www.paintmash
.com.) If you have a Mac, which does not come with a basic word processing program,
one popular freeware download is Neo Office, available at www.neooffice.org.

If you don't like Microsoft, try Adobe (although this is overkill for basic word processing needs).

Electronic Billing

If you send billings and other documents electronically to your clients, your software
will need to be compatible with theirs. If you have the most current version of Word,
for instance, and your clients do not, they will not be able to open the document
properly unless you send a copy in an earlier version of Word. Adobe Acrobat, on
the other hand, is universally readable. The standard edition of Adobe Acrobat 9 is
currently $299 from Adobe.

Google docs (docs.google.com), as mentioned earlier, offers basic word processing and spreadsheet programs for free. The documents you create stay stored
on Google's servers and can be saved under different formats on your hard drive.
The main benefit of Google docs is the ability for multiple users to work on the
same document simultaneously. This isn't a feature required by a handyman business, but if you're short on operating funds, Google docs is one way to get started
with some basic software to create your documentation. Google docs run on most,
but not all, browsers. Check their Web site to see if your browser is compatible.

Accounting Software

Before the advent of office computers, business owners did their books with handwritten ledgers and manual adding machines (imagine that). In my own very unscientific survey of used computers sold by individuals, when they are sold with software,
they more often come with Microsoft Office or something like Photoshop included
as opposed to any accounting software. The standard accounting software to beat
is QuickBooks from Intuit, which currently runs around $200. As a small business,
presumably with few or no employees, you do not need exotic accounting programs,

but can easily perform all your accounting functions with the basic versions of these programs. If you want to be really frugal about it, you can create Word docs with fields for different accounting functions (payments received, accounts payable, and so on) and total your figures with your computer's calculator.

Other accounting programs include Microsoft Office Accounting Professional ($200 currently) and Peachtree (starting at $70).

Accounting by Hand

It's perfectly acceptable and legal to do all handwritten entries in a record and accounting book using a quill pen and a bottle of ink, as Ebenezer Scrooge did in *A Christmas Carol*. The key is to keep accurate, up-to-date records and not misplace them.

Work/Repair Area

One bad habit small contractors get into is a lack of regular housekeeping when it comes to supplies and materials. One window repair contractor I knew ended up with duplicates of a number of tools because he couldn't find the original ones he had purchased. He ended up with several drills, multiple hammers, and so on because he refused to keep his stock in order. You're a handyman—build some shelves in the garage or storage shed and keep them clean!

The amount of storage space you'll need depends on the variety of jobs you do, but figure on shelving or cabinets for tools, paints and other finishes, wood trim, drywall compound, plaster patch, small plumbing parts, fasteners, and cleaners. You'll need a workbench for tool repairs and any customer repairs—chair refinishing, for instance—you do at home.

The key is not allowing your materials and tools of the trade to overwhelm you and your storage space. In the manufacturing world—at least, those companies that adopt Lean Manufacturing (basically, a system of efficient, quality production practices)—using a "5S approach" to organize your work space through standardized design is definitely the way to go. It works for Toyota, who developed it, and it will work for you, too.

What is 5S?

- *Sort*—Eliminate what's unnecessary from the work space, such as broken tools and scraps of material.
- *Set in Order*—Store the tools and materials you need in specific locations so they're easily found; basically, a place for everything and everything in its place.
- *Shine*—After elimination and putting things away, tidy up your work and storage area, and clean it on a regular basis (this includes your vehicle).
- *Standardize*—Figure out the best way to do your job in your work area, whether it's in your garage or a client's job site, and practice this regularly.
- *Sustain*—Keep up these practices on a daily basis.

Storing Materials

Store flammable materials such as paint thinner in well-ventilated areas. Keep them out of direct sunlight and away from appliances (water heaters, furnaces, or clothes dryers) that could ignite them. You might want to consider building a secure storage shed away from your house for these materials.

If you haven't already built a workbench and storage area, bear in mind that you will have to have sufficient wiring to run a 20 amp circuit for some power tools, as well as lighting.

Vehicle Storage

Your vehicle will take on a different role now. In addition to providing transportation, it will also store your tools. Do you currently have a secure place to park and lock it? A garage is ideal; a driveway is workable; and street parking is the least desirable. Consider renting a secure garage if you don't have off-street parking available. Plan on installing outdoor lights, perhaps with motion detectors, if you park in a driveway. It only takes one break-in and theft of your tools to set you back and cause unnecessary financial stress.

Office and Storage Considerations

LOCATION

Home

Rented space

Monthly rent budget: $ _____

FURNITURE

New

Used

SHELVING AND STORAGE

Desk and filing cabinet

Attached shelves or freestanding

TECHNOLOGY

Computer (PC, Mac, or Linux)

Desktop, new: $_____

Desktop, used: $ _____

Laptop, new: $ _____

Laptop, used: $ _____

Printer

Print-only: $ _____

Multifunction: $ _____

DSL, cable, or satellite connection

Monthly fee: $_____

Software—freeware or proprietary

Office suite: $ _____

Accounting: $ _____

Internet monthly fees: (ISP) $_____ (Hosting) $ _____

WORK/REPAIR AREA STORAGE

Workbench, shelving, vehicle parking

You've done your financial planning and estimated how much you think your new business will cost to get started. Now you have to work on:

- collecting the money due to you;
- paying your bills;
- securing a line of credit; and
- saving and investing.

When you worked for someone else, your cash flow was consistent (or should have been consistent). Every two weeks, typically, you received a paycheck. You knew how much you were getting. There were no surprises (unless the company went broke and rudely informed you by not paying your salary). You really didn't have to think about it or go to any effort to get paid, or to have money deposited in a 401(k).

It's different as an owner of a handyman business. Most people will pay you on time with checks, direct deposits, or credit cards that clear promptly. A few will take their time paying, and some won't pay at all unless you threaten legal action. Even then, you might not collect, or it could cost you far too much in time or legal fees to do so.

While you're collecting what's due to you, your creditors—suppliers, insurance companies, and those to whom you owe taxes—are trying to collect your money that's due to them. It's critical that you don't get behind in these payments. You want a reputation for paying on time and in full.

Finally, you want to get ahead financially and not just tread water. This means regular saving and investing (even when you don't want to, since it means delayed gratification, and that's almost anti-American). So what? Become a radical, question the authority of rampant consumerism, and put some money aside. There will be unending opportunities in your life to buy stuff you don't need. Right now, you're trying to establish an independent business, and you'll need money available for downtimes and emergencies.

Handyman and Collection Agency

The best time to collect the fees due to you are at the point of sale—that is, from your customer when you've finished a job. This is how most appliance technicians, plumbers, and other contractors doing small jobs get paid, and it's how it should be. I call this the "grocery-store model" of payment. When you buy groceries, you go to a checkout line, your food items get bagged up, and you pay what's due. There are no negotiations or IOUs or bills mailed to you.

Construction contractors doing larger jobs than the ones you'll be doing—kitchen remodels, new roofs, room additions—bill in stages. Even with down payments, they are often out some money for materials and labor before a bill gets paid. This is not a great position to be in, given the fact that if payment isn't made or there's a dispute, the contractor has already paid out and can't go back and undo the work.

How can you help ensure that payment is made at the end of each job?

- When first discussing the work with your client, note that payment is due upon completion; this information should be included in any estimate forms or contracts used in your business.
- Have a printed bill ready at the end of the job. You can print up your own using a software program and ink in the final prices, or use preprinted forms and fill in the job information. This allows for any changes that may have occurred since the original job description was written.
- Mention at the start of the job when you expect to be finished, and the fact that at that time, the job will be ready for customer inspection and payment.

Yes, paper checks are a dying form of financial transaction, but unless you and each customer are set up for electronic payments, you'll still be dealing with some checks. *Deposit all checks immediately, preferably with an actual teller.* Why? On *some* occasions, deposits in night depository boxes or ATMs get lost or misplaced by the bank. The fact that you have a receipt doesn't prove there was any check in the deposit envelope.

Paper Dollars

Some customers will pay in cash, which is both very quaint and very cool at the same time. Great, you think, a pile of $20 bills. It's tempting not to report these transactions, but legally you must. If you deposit these payments in your bank account, do so through a teller. Then there's no doubt that the deposit was made and recorded. You might keep this cash for pocket money in lieu of making a separate cash withdrawal, but be sure to record it as part of your "payments received."

Digital Dollars

Increasingly, at least with younger customers—I know, that's a broad generalization, but early users of new technology are most often those who grow up with it—electronic payments will be common and expected. You will have to set up your checking account online to receive electronic payments, or set up credit card accounts and be paid with a credit card directly with a scanner, or electronically (your mobile phone or PDA will make this possible, unless the client pays online). The credit card approach is more expense for you, but ensures faster payment, as do electronic payments to your bank from customers who are set up to pay this way. *Remember: Pay close attention to your online activity to avoid bank fraud!*

Snail-Mail Payments

Some payments will be made through snail mail and the U.S. Post Office, such as:

- final payments for jobs which took several days, or were stretched out over a longer period of time than one day;
- customers who will not be at the job site when you're there and for whom a bill must be left (or mailed) for payment; and
- repeat customers, such as property managers, who pay monthly or per job.

In these cases, do your best to estimate the arrival time of the payment, as this will affect your cash flow.

Regardless of whether you're paid with a paper check or electronic deposit, note that the payments will still take a period of time to clear! Check your bank's funds-availability schedule to confirm when the deposits have cleared.

How do you protect yourself against bad debts? Aside from using your best judgment when you meet new customers, and thinking, "Well, they seem okay; I'm not expecting any trouble with the bill," you have some legal recourse, including:

- a mechanic's lien;
- small claims court; or
- collection agencies.

Even in tough economic times, if a customer contracts with you for handyman services, you can expect most everyone will pay in a timely manner. However, there will always be the potential for someone to stiff you. This should be part of your assessment when you take on a new job, but it shouldn't completely cloud your decisions.

It's in the Mail . . .

Before resorting to any legal recourse described here, be sure to contact your client by mail or phone and inquire about the problem payment. Occasionally mail gets lost, or a customer thought a bill had been paid and instead was mistakenly ignored. Other times a client is unexpectedly short on cash and was too embarrassed to discuss it with you. These are not excuses, just reality, so contact the client to have a clear understanding of why the payment has been delayed.

Mechanic's Lien

A mechanic's lien is defined as the right of a craftsman, laborer, supplier, or other individual who has supplied materials or labor toward the construction or improvement of a parcel of real estate to place a lien or claim on that property for the value of the services and/or materials if they are not paid for in full. Each state has its own laws regarding mechanic's liens, including requirements for written notice to the property owner, limits on how much payment can be collected, and time limitations for filing the lien. Even if a general contractor has been paid by a property's owner, a mechanic's lien can still force the owner to pay a subcontractor or supplier if the general contractor has not been paying, or is in arrears.

Placing a lien does not guarantee that you will be paid all that's due to you, or even that you'll be paid soon. The lien stays attached to the property and must be satisfied before the property can be sold. A lien claimant can file a lawsuit to force the sale of the property in order to collect payment from the proceeds of the sale. On public projects, a lien typically does not attach to the real estate or buildings, but rather to a fund of money due from the public authority to the principal contractor.

Placing a lien is a last resort for getting paid, but it can be very effective. Property owners, especially owners of commercial property who are dependent on bank loans or investor money, do not want liens on their projects. A lien is a red flag to the bank that the owner isn't paying bills on time, and this makes the bank wonder what the owner is doing with its money. General contractors don't like liens, either, as it suggests they aren't managing the job professionally and may be contractually called on to file a bond to cover the lien claim.

If you decide to file a lien, be sure the amount of money and the potentially damaged business relationships are worth it to you. Minor disputes over money—you decide if it's minor or not—are hardly worth the trouble. If the amount owed you is substantial—you decide this as well—and you're not concerned about any future fallout from the customer, then by all means file the lien to protect yourself.

Before filing a lien, you must file a notice of intent or right to lien with the property owner. Sending a notice of intent or right to lien is not a hostile or distrustful act in the commercial contracting world, or in the home-building world, where the dollar amounts are substantial. You are simply protecting your rights, and you need to explain this to your client if you get a less-than-cheery reaction.

You will need to file this notice within the time frame noted in your state laws. Some states require you to send notice before furnishing any labor or materials, others prior to receiving your first payment, and others allow a window of time from the commencement of the job. The notice is simply saying to the owner, Hello, I'm here, and I expect to get paid in a timely manner. Notice should be delivered by certified mail with a signed return receipt requested. This provides written verification that your notice was received.

NOTICE OF INTENTION TO FILE A MECHANIC'S LIEN

TO: _____ (Property Owner)

_____ (Address)

Notice is hereby given that the undersigned, _____ (Name) intends to file a mechanic's lien for _____ Dollars ($), on real property owned by you and commonly known as _____ (Street Address).

The filing of this lien, pursuant to _____(Statute), is for securing payment of amounts due for _____(describe services) performed by the undersigned within the last _____(number) days, in accordance with the agreement entered into on _____(date) between you and the undersigned.

This filing of intent to lien is done solely as a good business practice for the protection of the undersigned and does not in any way indicate or suggest any expectation that our aforementioned agreement is jeopardized or otherwise in question.

Date_____ _____ (Signature)

Small Claims Court

Suing in small claims court and winning doesn't guarantee you'll be able to collect. You'll have to balance the value of the amount due to you versus the trouble of going to court and the additional work to collect on the debt if your client refuses to pay voluntarily. Small claims court only determines the merits of a claim; it does not facilitate claim collection. That said, solvent individuals and businesses are much easier to collect from than those who are not. Deadbeat clients have certain legal protections that prevent you from forcing the seizure and sale of certain assets, although wages can often be partially garnished.

Although the specific procedures for small claims court vary from state to state, the following are generally true:

- There is a limit to the amount of money you can claim (up to $5,000 seems to be a common figure).
- There will probably be a small filing fee.
- No lawyers are involved—just you and your ne'er-do-well customer.
- Each party presents its side; be sure to bring all evidence, including photos of the completed work, witnesses, and copies of the estimate and contract.
- The means of appealing a court decision vary.
- Small claims court can be a time-consuming experience. You'll get your day in court, but it will involve lost work time.

Collection Agencies

Collection agencies are third parties that collect unpaid debts for a fee (a percentage of the collected debt). They must follow the Fair Debt Collection Practices Act, which was created by the Federal Trade Commission to ensure that debtors are not subjected to harassing collection techniques. If your client can make a legitimate case for not paying you, or is bankrupt, hiring a collection agency won't get you very far. As gratifying as visions of big debt-collecting hulks visiting your customer and coming away with your pile of cash may be, collection agencies mainly use the telephone and mail to go after your money.

Before hiring a collection agency, try to write and phone your wayward client first. You can save yourself some money and possibly clear up a misunderstanding.

Your Turn to Pay

Paying your suppliers and creditors promptly isn't the same as paying them the day their billings arrive. Pay by the due date and keep your cash in your own accounts as long as possible. Even in days of low interest rates, every bit of return matters. By electronically transferring funds to your suppliers, you can maintain your cash to the very day it's due and still be timely in your payments.

Here is a normal payment timetable you can expect in your handyman business:

- Pay employees every two weeks unless otherwise agreed upon.
- Pay suppliers monthly.
- Taxes—income, sales, and business-related—are due approximately fifteen days after the end of each calendar quarter (April 15, July 15, October 15, and January 15).
- Federal payroll taxes (if you have employees) are due fifteen days after the payroll month in question (e.g., June 15 for May taxes) if you withhold $50,000 or less.
- Insurance payments are due monthly, quarterly, every six months, or once a year, depending on your payment schedule with your insurer.
- Surety bond payments to a bonding agency are paid once a year.
- If you are paying for a vehicle, payments are due monthly.

Although you should pay all your bills when they're due:

- Always pay your taxes on time! The government is less forgiving than vendors and other creditors, with whom you can often negotiate if you've run into a cash shortage.
- Contact your vendors and explain your situation.
- Silence or ignoring your bills is the worst thing you can do.
- Even if someone is delivering bad news, most of us would rather hear something than be left wondering why we're not being paid.

As you can see, a lot of people want money from you! The last thing you want to do is lose track of money that's coming and going.

Cash Flow

As a handyman, you'll have relatively small ongoing financial demands outside of your own salary and that of any employees. Larger businesses with hundreds or thousands of employees and products and warehouses can go out of business pretty quickly if debts and the ability to service them exceed income. What's the worst that can happen to you if you have a bad month or two?

- If you have put money aside for six months' worth (or more) of expenses, you can ride out the storm.
- As a sole proprietor, you can change your prices overnight to reflect a new economic reality.
- You can do jobs you previously avoided.
- Worst-case scenario: You can temporarily work for someone else if work is available.

Regardless of what situations you face in your business, you have to monitor your cash flow. Here are a few guidelines to follow:

- Always have cash available, the same way you have personal cash set aside for emergencies and living expenses should your business income hit a snag.
- Watch your cash balance, not just your monthly bank balance. Your daily cash balance will guide your decisions about whether to buy new equipment or take on certain jobs or work longer hours.

- Look ahead to upcoming expenses and project the cash flow needed to meet these expenses; this way, you'll have fewer surprises.
- Until you've spent at least a year in the business—and that's the bare minimum—don't assume every month's income or expenses will be the same.
- You can't predict the future, so stay conservative in your expectations and expenditures until your business is well established.

Conservative doesn't necessarily mean complete risk avoidance, but it does suggest calculated risk. You cannot completely avoid the uncertainty that comes with an independent business, but you can manage it if you act intelligently without climbing out to the end of the weakest limb available to you.

Bank Line of Credit

As much as I advocate avoiding unnecessary debt, having a line of credit available *for careful and judicious use* can be useful for managing temporary cash shortfalls or unexpected large expenses (replacing a vehicle, for instance). The time to arrange for a line of credit is when you *don't* need it so it's there when you *do* need it.

You have two main lines of credit open to you:

- Home equity line of credit
- Unsecured line of credit

A home equity line is based on the amount of equity you have in your home. The terms and rates vary with each lending institution. You draw off the credit line as needed using checks or a credit card tied to the loan. Generally, the interest paid is tax-deductible.

An unsecured line of credit is based on you and your business and your credit history, as interpreted by the lending institution. A business that's an ongoing concern offers more financial records for review. As a new business, the bank would look at your personal history and make a determination. In this latter case, you would probably have a better chance of securing a line of credit with a bank with which you've had a long-term account.

Taking Out a Loan

You *could* use your credit cards for quick cash loans, but it's a very expensive way to go and not recommended, despite all the stories of entrepreneurs and moviemakers who financed their projects this way. You hear about the successful outcomes, not the mountains of debt for failed projects.

A direct loan from your bank is questionable if you're a new business with no business credit history, but go ahead and inquire. If you need the cash in a hurry to tide you over for a month or so, it's unlikely a loan would go through fast enough for your needs.

Equipment Allowance

Of all people, you, the handyman, understand that equipment wears out and needs repair and maintenance. Even the best-made power tools eventually need new brushes or switches. Tools also get lost or misplaced, blades get dull, and screwdrivers, easily the most frequently abused tools, are used as scrapers, pry bars, and chisels, thus ruining them for performing the tasks they were designed to do: tighten and loosen screws. As you expand your job repertoire, you'll need some new tools.

How much should you allow for equipment upkeep and replacement? If you start out with a wide variety of tools, both hand and power, and they're in good shape, you'll only be replacing the occasional lost or ruined screwdriver, nail set, or paintbrush. Your work will probably be varied enough that you won't be running a sander or circular saw for days and days without end, which would shorten their work lives.

As a handyman, you'll do most of your own power-tool repairs and only pay for the parts. Replacing brushes in a Makita sander, for instance, only takes a few minutes, and the brushes are inexpensive. Power cords will fray or get cut and need occasional replacement, also inexpensive to do.

Unless your tools are stolen or you expect to purchase some expensive items—a table saw, for instance—at some point in the future, your equipment allowance should be fairly modest. A few hundred dollars per year would more than cover the scenario described here.

Vehicle Maintenance

You'll need a dependable set of wheels. Every day without your car or truck is a day without income and a day with annoyed customers you have to reschedule. Taking a day or two off to do your own vehicle repairs can be a false savings. Now is the time to line up a good mechanic and a rental car arrangement—Enterprise will come to you, always a big help—for those times when your vehicle unexpectedly gives out and you have customers waiting.

How much should you calculate for a year's vehicle maintenance? It depends on the year, make, and model of the vehicle, your expected mileage, and its overall condition. There are plenty of calculators for "true cost of ownership," but the results vary depending on the data behind the calculator. You can calculate the expected maintenance—oil changes, tire rotations, winterizing—by following the owner's manual's recommended maintenance schedule, but the rest will take some educated guessing based on your knowledge of your vehicle and its maintenance to date. If you're looking at a water pump replacement, a brake job, or a head gasket anytime in the near future, now is the time to start putting the money aside for these repairs.

■ Credit card	Fast, easy, but a service charge
■ Electronic transfer	Fast, service charges vary

When you'll get it:

■ At job completion	Standard time for payment
■ On account	Business clients
■ In the mail	By previous arrangement only
■ No payment after inquiry?	
■ Mechanic's lien	Requires notice to be served first
■ Small claims court	No lawyers, ties up your time, payment not guaranteed
■ Collection agency	Fee-based

Payments you owe:

■ Employees	Pay every two weeks unless otherwise arranged
■ Taxes	Quarterly payments for most taxes
■ Suppliers	Monthly payments
■ Insurance	Payments vary
■ Bond	Yearly payment if using a bonding agency

When you need cash:

■ Home equity loan	Establish in advance of need, use as reserve
■ Unsecured line of credit	Establish in advance of need, use as reserve
■ Credit cards	Expensive, use only as a last resort

Savings and Retirement

Congratulations on your new business. Now it's time to start putting some retirement money aside.

Even if you expect to be doing some type of work until you're very old, you should still open a retirement account and make regular contributions to it. Your notion of work and relaxation can change as you hit sixty-something, or you could be physically limited from working the way you do now. Take advantage of tax-deferred savings and open a retirement account.

If you're in your early twenties, this is actually the best time to do this even though it's the furthest thing from your mind. Why? Your investments have more years to earn a return than if you start later. According to www.msn.com's Money Central columnist Liz Pulliam Weston, "Someone who puts $4,000 a year into retirement accounts starting at 22 can have $1 million by age 62, assuming 8% average annual returns. Wait 10 years to start contributions, and you'd have to put in more than twice as much—$8,800 a year—to reach the same goal."

Can't swing $4,000? Any amount is better than nothing. Once you discover you can comfortably get by with a hundred or two hundred or three hundred fewer dollars a month that you've tucked away into a retirement or investment account, saving will become automatic.

You have a number of investment choices:

- Savings account
- Brokerage/investment account
- Contributory IRA
- Simple IRA
- SEP-IRA
- Roth IRA
- Individual 401(k)
- Keogh

You only have so much money to put aside, so consider your options carefully.

Savings Account

Savings accounts offer modest returns at best and are worthwhile for parking money temporarily. They are not long-term investment plans. Minimum start-up balances are pretty low, often $100, so it's easy to establish a savings account. Assuming your bank is protected by the FDIC (Federal Deposit Insurance Corporation), your savings will be insured up to $250,000 per depositor, per bank. The interest you earn will be taxed.

Not every financial product is FDIC-insured. According to the FDIC, the following are insured:

- Checking accounts (including money market deposit accounts)
- Savings accounts (including passbook accounts)
- Certificates of deposit

The following are not insured:

- Investments in mutual funds (stock, bond, or money market mutual funds), whether purchased from a bank, brokerage, or dealer
- Annuities (underwritten by insurance companies, but sold at some banks)
- Stocks, bonds, Treasury securities, or other investment products, whether purchased through a bank or a broker/dealer (Note: Treasury securities are not FDIC-insured, but they are guaranteed by the U.S. Government—meaning, the government would have to fail for the securities to lose value.)

A savings account is a start, but not the end of your financial planning.

Investment Strategies

Some investors do very well for themselves by buying real estate, primarily rental properties, and holding on to them forever, eventually living off the rents. This can be a sound strategy, especially for a handyman, but it's not very diversified, and as with every investment, problems can arise (rental markets soften, housing prices drop). Consider real estate as part of your portfolio, but not as your sole investment.

Brokerage/Investment Account

Stock markets go up and stock markets go down. In the long run, stocks are a good investment. They are purchased through a stock brokerage firm whose services range from full to do-it-yourself. Brokerage firms range from do-it-yourself to full-service, and some are associated with banks for one-stop shopping. When you open a brokerage account, your cash deposits are placed in a money market account—which is not insured—and this money is used to purchase stocks, bonds, mutual funds, certificates of deposit, and other investments. Returns are not guaranteed; you reap all the gains and suffer the losses, so tread thoughtfully here (read the most updated version of *The Intelligent Investor* by Benjamin Graham for starters). The money you earn through interest, dividends, and increased stock prices (realized once the stocks are sold) are all taxable; losses, once the losing investments are sold, are normally tax-deductible. Pretty much everyone who is wealthy in this country is invested in the market.

A Tip from a Pro

Warren Buffet, arguably one of history's most successful investors, has suggested that the average person would be wise to invest in an index mutual fund, which buys a basket of stocks broadly representing the market or large segments of it. The gains and losses will reflect the market at large and will therefore not be as great as the gains or losses of individual stocks. In other words, steady returns in the long run, and no guessing at which stocks are going to be the big winners. There are a lot of index funds; Vanguard (www.vanguard.com) funds are well regarded and have some of the lowest fees in the industry.

IRAs

IRA stands for "Individual Retirement Account." They were first introduced by Congress in 1974 and have since grown in variety and in the size of allowable contributions. The idea is to make tax-deferred contributions during your earning years and pay the taxes as you withdraw the money in retirement (the Roth IRA is the exception; see below).

You are in charge here; there is no company retirement plan handling your money for you or making matching contributions. If you don't fund an IRA or equivalent account, no one will. Sure, you'll have Social Security, and perhaps the money from the sale of a home, but Social Security was never meant to be enough money to live on. It was intended to be a supplement. Selling a house can provide a nice nest egg that then must be spent on another nest somewhere else.

IRAs come in several flavors:

- **Contributory IRA:** A traditional IRA allowing contributions of up to $5,000 per year if you're less than fifty years of age, and $6,000 if you're fifty or older.
- **SIMPLE (Savings Incentive Match Plan for Employees of Small Employers) IRA:** Allows you to contribute up to $11,500 (as of 2009), tax-deferred. If you employ 100 or fewer people earning at least $5,000 a year, they can join this plan, and you must make limited matching contributions for each participant. If you establish a SIMPLE IRA, you cannot have any additional plans to which you contribute.
- **SEP (Simplified Employee Pension) IRA:** Allows a contribution up to $49,000 out of a maximum income of $245,000. Your contribution for employees must match the same percentage contribution you make for yourself.
- **Roth IRA:** Accepts after tax dollars—that is, you've already paid your income taxes on the contributions. When you withdraw from the account, the money and its increased value is all tax-free. You can contribute up to $5,000 currently if you are less than fifty years of age, and up to $6,000 if you're over fifty.
- **Individual 401(k):** This is an option if you have no employees—it's just for you. You can contribute up to $46,000 if you are less than fifty years of age, or up to $51,000 if you are fifty or older. This plan is more complicated than an IRA and has higher setup fees.
- **Keogh plan:** Applies to unincorporated businesses and their employees. It's also more complicated than an IRA and comes with setup fees and maintenance costs. A Keogh is more than you need at this point.

You're thinking to yourself, If I had $46,000 a year to contribute to a retirement plan, you think I'd be opening a handyman business—or any other business, for that matter? Fair enough; so start small with one of the chosen IRA options. Your bank or a brokerage firm can open an account, usually for very modest fees or no fees at all, either to set up or maintain the account. There are rules about:

- withdrawals
- calendar dates by which time an account must be established and contributions made for an individual tax year
- spousal considerations
- income limits
- how you file your taxes (married filing jointly, single filer, etc.)
- employee contributions
- catch-up contributions (extra contributions you can make if you're fifty years of age or older)
- total contributions when you have multiple plans (i.e., Roth and Contributory IRAs together can total $5,000 or $6,000, depending on age, not $5,000 or $6,000 individually when you have both accounts)

There is no end to the amount of Web-based information available, all devoted to retirement plans, to help you choose the best for your circumstances. Your bank will also have information, albeit perhaps more marketing-oriented.

Can't decide? Start a Roth IRA. It's simple and uncomplicated. You can have multiple IRAs and start others later if you want to make larger contributions than a Roth allows. Keep in mind: There are penalties and taxes for most IRA withdrawals before age fifty-nine and a half (Roth IRAs have different rules), but there are provisions for borrowing money from a 401(k). These are not bank accounts in the normal sense, and are not used as collateral for loans.

The key considerations to financial planning in your handyman business aren't very different than those in your personal financial planning:

- Save some money.
- Avoid unnecessary debt.
- Look ahead and be ready for bills and taxes you know you'll have to pay on given dates.
- A little sacrifice never hurt anyone (much).
- Keep emergency money on hand, enough to live on for a few months (or longer).
- Invest something for the future, even if you're a nihilist.

Summary of Savings, Investments, and Retirement Plans

Passbook Savings / Bank Accounts

Pays minimal interest, guaranteed to $250,000 if bank is FDIC-insured.

Certificates of Deposit (CDs) and money market deposit accounts are also covered if bank is FDIC-insured.

Low minimum initial balance required to start an account.

Brokerage Account

Account is set up at a stock brokerage firm or through a bank which has a brokerage branch (e.g., Wells Fargo Bank, Bank of America).

Cash is held in money market mutual fund, which is not FDIC-insured, but normally pays higher interest than bank rates.

You can purchase, hold, and trade stocks, bonds, mutual funds, Treasury bills, and other investments (only Treasury bills and other government debt is guaranteed).

Historically, stocks offer higher returns, along with accompanying risks, than other investments.

Starting balance varies with individual brokerage firms.

IRA (Individual Retirement Account)

Various types of IRAs are available; most use tax-deferred income to fund them, and money is taxed upon withdrawal.

Accounts can be set up at brokerage firms or banks offering IRA services.

These accounts are self-directed, simple to set up, with no guaranteed returns.

They include the same investments you would have in a brokerage account.

Minimum starting balances vary with brokerage firm.

Depending on the type of IRA, your maximum yearly contribution will also vary.

Types of IRA accounts include:

Contributory

SIMPLE

SEP

Roth

Roth IRA is funded with after-tax dollars; money is not taxed upon withdrawal.

Other Retirement Accounts

Individual 401(k) is aimed at self-employed individuals; the plan is named for a section of the IRS Tax Code and allows for very generous contributions.

A Keogh is aimed at higher-income individuals and is more complex to set up than an IRA.

08 | Taxes and Recordkeeping

U.S. Supreme Court Judge Oliver Wendell Holmes Jr. has been quoted as saying, "I like paying taxes; with them, I buy civilization." This is quite true, but the process of preparing tax returns can be anything but civilized. This is one reason why tax preparation is a multibillion-dollar business.

The Internal Revenue Service and the appropriate state and local taxing authorities tax you on your income regardless of its source, including:

- Goods and services
- Interest and dividend payments
- Illegal activities

This last item might surprise you, but the tax code doesn't judge what you do to earn money—it just wants you to pay taxes on it. (It was tax evasion that finally landed gangster Al Capone in jail.) As a handyman, you will pay taxes on all the income left over after you've paid for supplies, materials, transportation, employee salaries, and other legitimate overhead. This isn't especially complicated; you just need to know the valid and acceptable deductions you can take, record them properly, and file the correct tax forms.

How you account for your income and expenses, cash or accrual, can affect how your taxes are done, but does not change the fact that your books should be accurate.

The Taxman Takes His Share

Taxable income includes any goods or services you receive through bartering; it isn't limited solely to cash. Some (too many) bartering advocates suggest otherwise, implying these are tax-free exchanges (i.e., you repair a plumber's deck and the plumber replaces a couple of your sinks). Bartering can't really be monitored so is infrequently reported, but reporting is legally required. Your bartering transactions are recorded on *Form 1099-B, Proceeds from Broker and Barter Exchange Transactions*. Use *IRS Publication 525, Taxable and Nontaxable Income*.

Cash Accounting vs. Accrual Accounting

CASH

- Records income when it's received
- Records expenses when you pay them
- Tells you how much cash you have in the bank, but not your true cash position

ACCRUAL

- Records income when the sale or job occurs, regardless of when you get paid
- Records expenses when they occur, even if you pay for them later
- More accurately matches income and expenses during the time period in which they occur, giving you a better picture of your company's financial health

With the cash method, you record figures once, when transactions actually happen. If you use accrual, you record an entry in an accounts receivable file and expenses in an accounts payable file. Later, when the money is actually received or paid out, you would record those transactions as well.

How does this work? Let's say you buy some lumber, nails, and plaster compound for $75 and put it on your account. You use the materials on a job, get paid $325, and off you go to the bank, feeling $325 richer. Not quite; you still have to pay for the materials. You're really ahead $250. A cash method of accounting won't reflect this—it will only show the $325 received. When you pay your bills some days or weeks later, then you'll account for the $75 in materials. For a sole proprietorship with no employees, no inventory, and a lot of short-term jobs, the cash method works fine—even if it provides a less-accurate cash picture. This assumes your jobs are profitable and you're prudent in your spending—that you don't "blow" all your income and not allow for paying for materials and overhead. If you need more accuracy because your money situation is tight, go with the accrual method.

Good Accounting and Recordkeeping Lead to Easier Tax Filing

A couple of my college professors were loose with their recordkeeping, and when it came time to graduate, they weren't quite up to speed with verifying class rosters with class completion. Fortunately, I kept copies of all my class registrations and could show I had both enrolled and completed the classes. Let's just say it was a very liberal arts school and recordkeeping wasn't a universal strong point.

You have to record money in and money out; it's as simple as that. Otherwise, you'll have a hard time keeping track of your profitability and paying the correct amount of taxes. Some people are thrilled when they get a big tax refund. A tax refund is simply an interest-free loan made to the IRS. Who would be thrilled about that?

You know from chapter 5 that accounting software is available, along with paper-based ledgers for keeping track of money. With either system:

- Record all expenses and customer payments as they occur—it's too easy to toss a receipt aside and forget the box of bathroom tile you purchased.
- Regularly reconcile all electronic records with paper receipts and billings.
- Store all paper receipts and paper copies of contracts and billings.
- Make copies of all tax forms and file them.

Storage Tips

One convenient way to store paper is in three-ring binders. Buy a three-hole punch at any office supply store, punch the paper as needed, and store by year (or by other category).

How long should you keep all this paper? Use the following guidelines:

ITEM:	HOW LONG TO KEEP:
Accounts payable/ receivable	10 years
Audit reports	Indefinitely
Bank statements	3 years
Canceled checks	10 years
Important canceled checks (i.e., taxes)	Indefinitely
Contracts	10 years
I-9 Documents	3 years after date of hire or one year after terminination, whichever is greater
Legal correspondence	Indefinitely
Tax returns	Indefinitely
Financial ledgers/records	Indefinitely
Deposit slips	2 years
Payroll records	10 years
Personnel files	10 years
Retirement and pension records	Indefinitely

This is on the conservative side. It's a handyman business, not a human vaccine testing lab or securities trading. If you file your taxes electronically, all the easier to keep copies on a hard drive or other storage media. If you run your business properly, pay your bills and taxes on time, and avoid unfair dismissal suits with employees, all your stored records will probably end up in a corner of your basement or garage gathering dust.

Update Your Electronic Media

Be sure to update your electronic storage records as the storage media changes. CDs and flash drives will eventually go the way of floppy disks, so pay attention as the technology advances. Otherwise, you could find yourself years down the road with media you can't read unless you go to a service that, for a price, will open your old files using outdated hardware.

Filing Tax Returns

If you work alone and expect to owe $1,000 or more in federal income taxes, you'll have to file estimated taxes quarterly, or every three months. The tax system is pay as you go. Employees have taxes removed with every paycheck. You have to estimate your yearly tax payment and pay it off in four installments. You have to guess as best you can for your first year in business. Underpay too much and you might be subject to a penalty; overpay and you get a refund. After your first year in business, you can base the next year's payments on the previous year's taxes, sometimes referred to as "prior year safe harbor." The other alternative, if your income increases, is to try and estimate 90 percent of the current year's taxes. Most people choose to use the previous year's total, although this could stick you with a large tax bill when you file your end-of-the-year return. You can mitigate this by paying more with each of your quarterly payments (on or about the fifteenth day of January, April, June, and September).

What if you earn substantially less one year than you did the previous? Adjust your payments accordingly. You want to be as close to the actual amount owed as possible without overpaying or underpaying a large amount.

There are fifty different sets of state income tax and business-related tax regulations to follow, so they cannot all be accounted for here. These will also be filed quarterly.

Who You Are Determines Which Forms to Use

A sole proprietorship is the simplest business from accounting and tax perspectives. The following IRS tax forms are associated with sole proprietorship businesses:

- *Form 1040 (Individual Income Tax Return)*
- *Schedule C: Profit or Loss from Business (or Schedule C-EZ)*
- *Schedule SE (Self-Employment Tax)*
- *Form 1040-ES (Estimated Tax for Individuals)*
- *Form 4562 (Depreciation and Amortization)*
- *Form 8829 (Expenses for Business Use of Your Home)*
- *W-4s* and *Form 940* (if you have employees)

A partnership is a bit more involved. The following IRS tax forms are pertinent to partnerships:

- *Form 1065 (Partnership Return on Income)*
- *Form 1065 K-1 (Partner's Share of Income, Credit, Deductions)*
- *Form 4562 (Depreciation)*
- *Form 1040 (Individual Income Tax Return)*
- *Schedule E (Supplemental Income and Loss)*
- *Schedule SE (Self-Employment Tax)*
- *Form 1040-ES (Estimated Tax for Individual)*
- *W-4s* and *Form 940* (if you have employees)

An LLC or Limited Liability Company is more complicated, naturally. As a sole owner of an LLC, you can use the same tax forms as a sole proprietorship. The LLC itself does not pay any taxes or file a return with the IRS. If you have co-owners, the IRS treats the LLC as a partnership, and the same forms are filed as for a partnership. Sole owners or co-owners can choose to file as a corporation, however, depending on how the LLC was formed. In that case, you'll need the following IRS tax forms:

- *Form 1120 or 1120-A: Corporation Income Tax Return*
- *Form 1120-W, Estimated Tax for Corporations*
- *Form 8109-B Deposit Coupon*
- *Form 4625 Depreciation*
- *W-4s* and *Form 940* (if you have employees)
- Other forms as needed for capital gains, sale of assets, alternative minimum tax, etc.

As you can see, the further you move up in the business world, the more complicated the tax returns.

Get Schedule C from:

www.irs.gov/pub/irs-pdf/f1040sc.pdf

Get form 1040 ES, the payment voucher section from:

www.irs.gov/pub/irs-pdf/f1040es.pdf

Reducing Your Taxes with Deductions

There are plenty of legitimate tax deductions available to you through your handyman business:

- Office overhead and expenses (everything from your telephone costs to office supplies to the purchase of a desk)
- All the supplies and materials used in the course of your repair work, such as paint, sandpaper, caulk, light switches, etc.
- Your automobile or truck expenses as they relate to your work. For instance, you can deduct the cost of driving to and from jobs, picking up supplies, or giving estimates. Any personal use of the vehicle during non-work hours is not deductible.
- All employee-related costs, including wages, training, and paid benefits
- Professional services (legal and accounting, for instance, including tax preparation)
- Repairs, maintenance, and tool replacement
- Rent on office or storage space
- Insurance
- License and bond
- One-half of your FICA or self-employment tax

> ### Keeping Vehicle Business Expenses Separate
>
> The easiest way to keep the business and personal vehicle expenses separate is to maintain a mileage log (either paper or electronic) where you note the miles driven for work. The IRS will allow 55 cents per mile deduction for 2009, although you can choose to deduct your actual expenses for gasoline, repairs, tolls, parking, etc., instead of a mileage deduction. Total up each at the end of the year and pick the greater deduction.
>
> These are all proper expenses and easily confirmed should the IRS ever require proof. Proof will be in the form of well-kept records and clear documentation.

About That Office Deduction . . .

Deducting your *physical home office*, as opposed to deducting office expenses, raises a red flag with the IRS. You can always deduct any business-related office expenses, such as your phone, computer, paper, and so on. You can also deduct the physical space itself, if you meet IRS requirements. These deductions can include a percentage of utility bills, mortgage interest, repairs, and depreciation, and are reported on IRS *Form 8829, Expenses for Business Use of Your Home*. You'll find this inside *Publication 587, Business Use of Your Home*, which will help you determine if your home office meets the IRS requirements.

What are the IRS requirements? Your home office:

1. must be used exclusively and regularly for business, including administrative and management activities which are not primarily conducted elsewhere; and
2. it must be your principal place of business, or be used to meet with clients or customers during the normal course of business.

If you have a separate structure, such as a detached cottage, it's much easier to meet the home office deduction requirements. A structure or space that's used for storage or repair work is also a viable deduction. As most of your time will be spent outside the office, and therefore little of your business will be done in the office, it will be tough to justify the deduction.

Section 179

Certain business property—computers, power tools, vehicles—have a useful life of more than one year. The IRS allows you to deduct these as expenses, but normally they are *depreciated* over several years (three years, five years, seven years, ten years, fifteen years, and twenty years, depending on the property and applicable depreciation schedule). You are allowed to deduct a certain percentage of the purchase price every year until the property is completely written off.

Thanks to IRS Code Section 179, you can completely deduct qualified property costing up to $133,000 (that covers a really big computer) if purchased in 2009. This provision applies to sole proprietors, partnerships, and corporations. Eligible property includes:

- Office equipment and furniture
- Machinery and tools
- Most storage facilities
- Business vehicles weighing between 6,000 and 14,000 pounds ($25,000 deduction; lower deduction for smaller vehicles)

Section 179 is a very useful tax tool, so use it to its fullest availability. Note that it cannot be used to reduce your taxable income below zero, although it would be lovely if it could. See IRS *Form 4562 Depreciation and Amortization and Instructions for Form 4562* for further information.

Audits

If your return falls within a normal pattern of deductions for a business and income of its type, as determined by computer analysis, it's not likely you'll ever get audited. In 2007, the audit rate for individual returns was approximately 1 percent.

Returns that fall outside of the norm include:

- Large amounts of itemized deductions
- Large business expenses in relation to income
- Home office deductions

The possibility of an audit is another compelling (more than compelling, actually) reason to keep good records and a neat accounting system. Even the IRS makes mistakes, so don't assume that notice of an audit means you're in the wrong.

Do It Yourself or Hire a Tax Service?

Some tax returns are a challenge, but many taxpayer fears of working on their own returns are unfounded. Yes, the tax code is complicated and written by lawyers, but most of it does not apply to you or the average taxpayer. Besides, it's a good mental exercise to do your own taxes. Too many people flock to tax preparation services for fairly simple returns.

You basically have four options for doing your taxes:

- Reconcile all your records, use a calculator, and manually fill out the return.
- File electronically using the IRS Free File program (www.irs.gov/efile).
- Use tax preparation software.
- Hire a tax preparation service, which can include a CPA or certified public accountant.

Regardless of how your taxes are prepared, you'll need all your records. If you've kept up your books, you'll have monthly totals for income and expenses readily available, and you won't have to bother with fishing paper receipts out of a shoe box. Increasingly, taxpayers are using software programs to prepare their taxes, and with good reason. Tax preparation software produces:

- Neat, easy-to-read returns
- More assured accuracy
- State and federal tax forms

TurboTax (www.turbotax.com) is the most popular tax preparation software, and is available in several editions for business taxes starting at around $100 from Intuit, and probably less from resellers. Are there other programs? Sure, including the low-cost Tax Act series from Second Story Software (www.taxact.com), but TurboTax is the elephant in the tax preparation room and is worth the extra cost.

Hiring It Out

You'd rather be patching walls and estimating jobs than doing your taxes? It will come at a price (the fee is tax-deductible, however), which varies depending on the complexity of your return and whether you file a state income tax return or not. The figure quoted by the National Society of Accountants for the average cost of preparing a Form 1040 with itemized deductions and one state form is $205. Although this figure is several years old, it's still regularly referenced. With your additional business-related tax forms, your fees, through an accountant, will be higher in many parts of the country.

Do you need a CPA? At this point, no; your business is pretty simple and straight-forward. Instead of a more-expensive CPA, you could consider:

- a tax preparation service, such as the ubiquitous H&R Block;
- an Enrolled Agent—a federally authorized tax practitioner who can do tax work and represent clients before the IRS in the event of an audit;
- other authorized practitioners, including attorneys and actuaries; or
- unlicensed tax preparers.

Tax laws change regularly. My former accountant called these changes "Tax Accountant Welfare and Benefits Acts," as they assured them continual business. (He was the same accountant who jokingly said he would defend a client's claims before the IRS to the client's "very last dime." I was not amused.) These changes are stated in your tax returns (changes in different allowances or deductions, for instance), so you can't entirely base the way you prepare one year's return on the way you prepared the previous year's return.

All tax preparers are not created equal, as pointed out in a February 19, 2008, *Smart Money* article, titled "10 Things Your Tax Preparer Won't Tell You." Noting the unequal and sometimes nonexistent training standards, the high error rate as discovered by the Government Accountability Office and the IRS, and regular incompetence among hired tax preparers, you have to wonder how much better off you are hiring this work out. Tax preparers use software, too, greatly simplifying their work—a process you can do yourself. Others outsource returns (to India, for instance), at a reduced cost to them, while you're still billed at the preparer's regular rate.

What should you do other than blindly pick a preparer? Talk with other small business owners and get a recommendation. You'll want someone who's established and is available year-round, not just during tax season. You'll want to know the preparer's background, continuing education, and rates. Get booked early! If you wait until April to have your taxes done, you're on your own.

For more information, go to the National Association of Tax Professionals and download their brochure, *Finding the Right Tax Preparer* (www.natptax .com/2005findataxprobrochure.pdf).

Employees

If you have employees when you start up your business, or expect to have them later, here are some things you need to know regarding taxes and recordkeeping:

- Keep track of hours and dates worked.
- Deduct and account for all federal and state taxes per pay period.
- Deduct and account for any voluntary payroll deductions, including health insurance premiums and retirement plan contributions.

Tax deductions include:

- Federal income tax withholding (see IRS Publication 15)
- Federal Insurance Contributions Act (FICA) withholding—6.2 percent by the employer and 6.2 percent by the employee
- Medicare withholding (1.45 percent of wages paid by the employer and 1.45 percent by the employee)
- Federal unemployment taxes (FUTA)
- State unemployment taxes (SUTA)
- State income tax withholding (if applicable)
- Any local tax withholdings (city, county, state disability, etc.)

As the employer, you must collect all these taxes, record them, be sure they reconcile with the employees' salary and working hours, and then send the taxes along to the appropriate government agency while filing all payroll tax returns.

To file the returns, you will use the following forms:

- *Form 940* or *Form 940EZ* for annual federal unemployment taxes
- *Form 941,* the employer's quarterly payroll tax return
- *Form 945, Annual Return of Withheld Federal Income Tax*
- *Wage and Tax Statements* or *W-2*
- *Form 8109, Federal Tax Deposit Coupon* (accompanies *Form 941*)
- Appropriate state and local tax forms

All of these forms are available at your state treasurer's office and from the IRS, at www.irs.gov.

You can spend a lifetime speaking about ethics. Combine ethics and legal matters—what's legal isn't always considered ethical—and a lifetime might not be enough. Many tie ethics to a power outside of themselves, often religious-based, while others view ethics as more of a supreme personal and social standard to live by. Either way, your handyman business will involve both legal and ethical issues, many of them ultimately based on money and its myriad temptations.

Money takes on many personalities. It's the root of all evil and the bearer of great generosity. No matter how much you have, you often want more. If you feel you don't have enough, there are plenty of people who have less. The whole idea of money—these pretty pieces of paper with numbers on them and the faces of long dead presidents and their friends—has made our lives a lot easier and more orderly. We love receiving money and often hate paying it out, and there's the rub.

As a self-employed handyman, it's up to you to provide a good level of service for the fees you charge. You will have plenty of opportunities to cut corners and oftentimes no one would ever be the wiser—at least until a repair prematurely fails, at which point you'll be long gone. It's tempting, especially if you've underbid a job or it's taking longer than you expected and it's past your dinnertime and you're still wrestling with a repair.

This is where you must maintain an ethical stand and follow the often-quoted golden rule of doing unto others as you would have them do unto you. This is a truism regardless of your personal beliefs, and in everyone's best interest. The world would be a much better place if we all kept this in mind during our social and business dealings.

You won't have a supervisor or manager watching over you (although the occasional customer might watch). Many (if not most) of your work situations will be you, working alone, so it's up to you to keep it honest and fair.

Ethics Do Pay Off

In 1982, Johnson and Johnson was faced with product tampering after seven people died from ingesting cyanide-tainted Tylenol. Within a few days, the company withdrew all Tylenol from the market, including previously sold product, at the cost of over $100 million, and created new safety packaging. These measures, guided by the company's belief that a customer should not be harmed by their products, went far beyond what was legally required. As a result, Tylenol eventually gained more market share than prior to its recall, and the drug industry developed more tamper-resistant packaging.

Legal Requirements

Legally, the actions you must follow are fairly clear:

- Maintain your license, insurance, and bond.
- If you have employees, follow all mandated hiring and firing practices (see appendix A).
- Report your income in full.
- Pay your taxes.
- Pay your vendors.
- Perform the work as per your contracts and agreements.
- Properly dispose of any toxic waste products and debris.

You cannot claim to be licensed, insured, and bonded if you're not. It's illegal. Besides, a clever customer will check up on you by going to the state government's Web site and searching under licensed contractors. You also cannot allow your license to lapse and still present yourself as licensed. Unlicensed handymen advertise all the time in neighborhood and weekly newspapers, as well as craigslist.com and similar Web sites. Some laws mandate a contractor's license number appear in the contractor's advertising.

Policies and Procedures

For your own protection and for the benefit of your employees, you should have your policies and procedures in some kind of printed format, most commonly in an employee handbook. Policies and procedures include:

- Safety procedures
- Reasons for termination
- Drug and alcohol rules
- Smoking restrictions
- Normal working hours
- Company holidays and personal days off
- Definition of harassment or unacceptable behavior
- Dress and hygiene code

Check with your state employment or Labor and Industries office regarding the legal necessity of an employee handbook or other written version of your policies and procedures. Even if one isn't required, you'll want to codify, in writing, your rules to avoid any legal problems later ("I was told I could wear a swimsuit and sandals to work. I did and I got fired.").

Employees

As noted in appendix A, employees have differing degrees of legal protection when hired and fired. If nothing else, you want to avoid any grief for yourself by not causing any grief for an employee. Even if a "wrongful dismissal" or "refusal to hire" suit is unfounded, you can still get caught up in one. Familiarize yourself with the laws and keep in mind how you would want to be treated in a similar situation.

One rule no one gets around concerns the *Form I-9, Employment Eligibility Verification*, which documents that each new employee is eligible to work in the United States. This rule went into effect April 3, 2009. For a copy of this form, go to www .uscis.gov/files/form/I-9.pdf. This is a Department of Homeland Security requirement for employment.

An employee handbook states your company's policies and procedures for how you conduct business and what you expect from your staff. The handbook should clearly state what you expect from an employee and what an employee can expect from the company. The handbook can become central to certain legal disputes if a policy is ambiguous or poorly written. It's advisable to have an attorney review the handbook before distributing it.

Your handbook does not have to overwhelm with details, but should have enough to avoid any misunderstandings. An Internet search on "writing an employee manual" will yield plenty of information on what to include, as well as companies that sell templates for writing your own handbook and those that will write one for you. Your handbook cannot include anything illegal, such as discriminatory practices. For a free partial template, as well as full templates for sale, go to http://hrit.com/.

Your handbook should include:

- an employee acknowledgment form, which, when signed and turned in by an employee, attests that the manual was both read and understood; and
- An Equal Employment Opportunity Statement.

Listed policies should include:

- Maintaining up-to-date employee personnel information
- Attendance
- Dress code
- How and when company property can be used
- Health and safety rules and violations
- Alcohol, drug, and other substance abuse
- Performance reviews
- Hourly and salaried status designations
- Compensation and benefits
- Payroll
- Vacation, holidays, and sick leave
- Medical, family, and sick leave
- Personal time off (PTO)

cont.

cont.

- Maternity leave
- Bereavement or funeral leave
- Military duty
- Jury duty
- Insurance issues
- Group benefits
- Disability
- COBRA (continuation of medical benefits)
- Workers' compensation
- Other benefits as appropriate

Income and Taxes

This formula is simple: You earn money, allow for deductions, and pay your taxes on whatever is left over, all the while following the fine tradition of paying as little as legally necessary. Whatever you earn is subject to taxes, but, depending on your income and deductions, you could end up with no federal tax liability at all and still be perfectly legal.

How?

Marlys Harris, *Money* magazine senior editor, tells of a technical writer in a March, 27, 2008, article who voluntarily reduced his income from about $100,000 a year to $29,000 in 2007 by becoming self-employed. After contributing to a health savings account, a SEP IRA, an individual IRA, deducting half of his self-employment tax (you can do this, too) and health insurance premium, he took a standard deduction and one exemption on his Form 1040. At that point, he owed no federal taxes. Granted, this writer lives a frugal life, but he manages to do it in San Francisco, one of the country's most expensive cities.

If such frugality doesn't interest you, bear in mind that your income will be taxed, including:

- Cash income
- Market-value equivalent of trading and bartering

Just because there's no bank transaction doesn't mean taxes aren't due.

Cash

It would be more than naive to say cash payments aren't tempting. The underground cash economy accounts for billions of dollars' worth of goods and services, none of which are taxed. Also, a client paying in cash might expect that you won't charge any sales tax.

This is one of those moments of parental admonition: Just because everyone else is doing it doesn't mean you should. Treat cash like any other taxable income.

Finders Keepers . . . Not

Occasionally, hidden money, buried inside a wall or floor, is discovered while working on a home. Far less occasionally, it's a huge amount of money. A contractor found $182,000 in Depression-era cash during a 2007 Cleveland-area remodel. A legal riot ensued between the contractor, who claimed some of the money, the homeowner, and the previous owner's legal heirs. If you find any cash, jewels, or original copies of the Gettysburg Address, hand it over to your customer.

Trade and Bartering

If you barter or trade services for other services or goods, the IRS expects you to pay taxes on the fair-market value of the services/goods received. Refer to *Publication 525, Taxable and Nontaxable Income* for additional information.

Contracts Count

An oral agreement isn't worth the paper it's not written on.

Is this too cynical? Not necessarily; but it's best for you and your clients if you have written confirmation or contracts for any work you propose to do. We all forget conversations or can easily misinterpret something that's said. Such lapses can be perfectly innocent, or part of a pattern of abusive claims ("I never agreed to that!"). An oral discussion, of course, is critical to establishing the outline of a job, but a written follow-up seals the deal. Keep your contracts clear and follow them to the letter. If you state that you will apply two coats of paint, then apply both coats, not one thick one and try to call it good. In essence, a deal's a deal, and just as you expect your client to live up to certain obligations, you are expected to do the same.

"I'll Trade You a Catered Dinner for Four if You Patch My Ceiling."

What constitutes a trade? Anything you can imagine. You can swap glass repair for auto repair from a mechanic. Does your favorite pub need the top of its bar refinished? You can trade for an open-ended tab until the dollar value of your refinishing has been consumed in brews and burgers. People trade all the time. Working for money is a trade as well. You trade time and services for currency that is then traded elsewhere for time and services you require. All money does is allow for more options. Otherwise, we would each have to search out others for our specific needs and hope they wanted what we were offering for trade in return.

Trades are negotiated by time (three hours of my time for three hours of your time), task (paint a bedroom in exchange for a plumber installing a sink and toilet), or cash equivalence. Cash seems to be the most straightforward. If you figure your time is worth $50 an hour and the job will take five hours, you'll expect $250 worth of trade in return.

How you set up the trade is your business, but you must account for it and pay taxes on its equivalent dollar amount.

Speed Memos

What happens if you're on the job, the contract signed, and your client asks you to do additional work or change the scope of the original agreement? Here's where a low-tech paper form can be very helpful. *Speed memos* or *rapid memos* are multipage carbon forms which allow you to write up change orders in the field and get them signed off by your customer. They are basically extensions to your contract and are available at office supply stores.

Hourly Fees

Some jobs will be bid as time and materials. You'll provide an approximate cost estimate, but because of the nature of the job—suspected but unconfirmed wood rot, for instance—an exact price isn't feasible. You need to keep an accurate accounting and bill accordingly. Your time can include picking up materials, clean-up, debris disposal, and all the other steps typically included in set-price estimates, but not breaks and lunch. If it looks like the job will run substantially over your estimate, always let the customer know before you get in too deep.

Client Confidentiality

There is no legally binding handyman/client confidentiality law that I'm aware of—unless you're also a practicing mental health therapist and your repair work is considered therapy, but that's a big stretch. You will meet a variety of people in your business as you work in their homes, some of which will be beyond immaculate and others seemingly impossible to move around in. Your clients will, to varying degrees, display their housekeeping, personal beliefs, health habits, sexual tendencies, and mental/emotional states to you. A few will be anxious for adult conversation, while most will leave you alone as you go about your job.

In the course of my work, my clients have included:

- A psychiatrist who needed a psychiatrist
- An exotic dancer with a few tales to tell
- A Valium addict for whom the Valium was no longer doing the job, as most communication involved screaming
- A chain-smoker who rarely opened her windows and whose apartment walls had turned yellow and brown
- A formerly homeless man who kept a daily, detailed list of possible thefts of his things by others living in his building, even though nothing was ever taken

You will have *some* clients like these, but *most* will be average working people such as you. All deserve their privacy. Will you talk about certain clients to your spouse or friends? Yes, of course; it's natural, as is any small talk or idle conversation. Talking is fine, but naming names (when the comments are negative about personal habits, for instance) is not. It's one thing to tell a fellow handyman to avoid Mr. Jones because he doesn't pay his bills, and quite another to reveal that he secretly cross-dresses. This isn't anyone else's business, and you'll be expected to keep it to yourself.

Up Close and (Too) Personal?

During the course of your work, you'll meet quite a few new people. Some might become friends, and this is normal. Many of our social contacts are made on the job. If you were to believe the reported myths and realities of some of the social interactions between male contractors and female customers, often homemakers (other combinations are certainly possible, but this one is more common), they easily go beyond just being newly discovered pals.

You *might* have a client *sometime* who's looking for more than deck repairs when deck repairs were the contracted job. It can be an appealing fantasy, but like all fantasies, the reality can be more like a Grimm's fairy tale. What two consenting adults decide to do with each other is generally their own business, but it can get messy—especially when there's an uncompleted business relationship in progress (What are the chances you'll want to finish the job after an afternoon tryst?).

To keep things professional:

- If you feel a customer is making inappropriate or uncomfortable suggestions or is dressed inappropriately, if not manipulatively, address it then and there.
- Leave the job if it's getting too awkward.
- Should you sense a mutual interest, you can always pursue a closer relationship after the job is finished.

This is a somewhat unexpected conversation for a "how-to" book, but unwelcome sexual situations are not unheard of between contractors and customers when alone at a customer's home. Even innocent flirting, *by a customer or by you*, can lead to problems. You need to be aware of the possibility and deal with it responsibly.

Smile, You're on Candid Camera

You want to know the best way to behave on a job? Assume you're on camera; better yet, a live cam so everything you do is being streamed online. Some clients *will* have security or nanny cams running. It's easy to "make yourself at home" when your client is out and you have the place to yourself. Contractors and their workers have been known to help themselves to cold drinks, aspirin from the medicine cabinet, or a hand tool from the garage. It's one thing when you're given permission to help yourself to a cup of coffee, or to grab a soda from the refrigerator; otherwise, it's hands off.

A Few More Job Concerns

Some jobs require permits.

- Any electrical work which adds a load to a circuit (an additional light or receptacle, for instance) typically requires a permit and inspection.
- The same is true for plumbing.
- Adding to or altering a weight-bearing wall will require a building permit, as will any major foundation work.

Rules vary, so if you're not certain, talk with your local building department. If you alter the electrical system without a permit and a malfunction results, causing a fire and related damage, there will be no end to your troubles. It's doubtful you could even get a permit to do some of these jobs without being licensed in the relevant specialty.

Work is done all the time without required permits. This doesn't mean it's a good idea. I've seen the results of uninspected electrical work, and some were quite ugly and unsafe. One contractor I knew had been asked by a homeowner to finish a deck he had started and had mostly completed. The contractor took one look and told him point by point why he would have to rebuild it completely, as it wasn't properly sized or assembled. In fact, collapsed upper-story decks periodically make the national news; inevitably, they were built incorrectly and without permits or inspections.

This is work you'll either want to avoid or go ahead with, as long as it's properly permitted.

Substituting Materials

When you bid a job and specify certain materials—Douglas fir studs, for example—your customer is expecting these materials to be used, even if they're hidden inside a wall and will never be seen. You can't bill for one material and then use a less-expensive one simply because your customer can't tell the difference. Substituting is acceptable if you clear it with the customer first, or write in a clause in the contract allowing for substitutions.

One way to avoid a conundrum over materials is to be as generic as possible in your contracts when specifying the materials isn't critical. There's little reason to identify the species of wood 2x4s you intend on using—just say you'll install 2x4s every 16 inches on center, as per standard building code. With finish materials, notably paints, the brand name will make a difference to many people, especially those who research them online, so these should be specified in many cases.

Waste—Toxic and Otherwise

Most jobs will produce some kind of debris and trash, anywhere from packaging scraps to lead-based paint dust. You should be clear with your client about how you intend to dispose of these leftovers. Few people will care if you toss a small amount of job-related trash out with the household trash. Others will take less kindly to your leaving a pile of scrap lumber from the wall you just demolished. You should state in your estimate and contract how debris will be disposed of, and bill accordingly.

What about toxic paints, thinners, and solvents? You have a few strategy choices:

- Mix all paint odds and ends of similar type in five-gallon buckets and use the resulting product (often it will be beige, gray, or a shade of brown) to paint sheds or other utility areas.
- Pour all used thinners into a two- or three-gallon container, allow the contaminant to sink to the bottom, and carefully pour the clear thinner into a clean container. Use this thinner for cleaning brushes and rollers, and recycle again.
- Save up these products and take them to a recycling center (sometimes local communities sponsor such recycling every few months).

It's easy, but unacceptable, to toss this waste in the trash. Do the right thing and either reuse or recycle.

Lead-Based Paint

It's safe to assume older homes, roughly anything built up until the 1950s, have some lead-based paint in them. Homes built up until 1978, when residential lead-based paint was banned, could have lead-based paint as well, but given the popularity of latex paint from the 1950s onward, it's much less likely than in homes built in earlier decades. Drilling through a wood casing that was once coated with lead-based paint is not a cause for concern, while tearing down a plaster wall requires precautions.

Federal law requires that you follow certain lead-abatement procedures if you do either of the following in a home, school, or child-care facility built before 1978:

- Renovate more than 6 feet of interior space
- Renovate more than 20 square feet of exterior space

After April 2010, the Environmental Protection Agency (EPA) requires the following:

- You must be certified in lead-abatement procedures (www.epa.gov/fedrgstr/ EPA-TOX/2008/April/Day-22/t8141.pdf).
- If you have employees, they must be trained to follow protective lead-safe work-practice standards (www.epa.gov/lead/pubs/rrpfactsheet2008.htm).
- Before starting a job, you must provide the homeowner with a copy of *Renovate Right: Important Lead Hazard Information for Families, Child Care Providers, and Schools* (www.epa.gov/lead/pubs/rrpamph.pdf). (Note: Providing this pamphlet is also a current requirement.)

Although these laws are mainly aimed at painters, general contractors, and window installers, they will affect you if your work involves any disturbance of lead-based paint, especially through demolition or sanding. In certain lead-aware cities—Boston and San Francisco come to mind—lead abatement is a big deal, and more closely monitored than in other areas.

Proper Waste Disposal

Lead-based paint debris can normally be disposed of in household trash on a residential job. Be sure to check with your local solid waste disposal organization for accurate information, as the rules can vary from one area to another.

When It's About You

A new customer has certain expectations of you. It is expected that you will be competent, honest, show up on time, keep a clean worksite, and try as best as possible to finish when you expect to finish. Most people will understand if a job takes longer than expected, provided it isn't way longer because you're in over your head. When a job is beyond your skill level or is new to you, and you think you can do it, be honest with your customer. It's hardly fair for you to bill for three hours as you learn on the job when someone else could complete it in one-third the time.

However, if your customer is comfortable with you doing it anyway, that's appropriate because the customer is making the decision with clear knowledge of the situation. Some handymen will reduce their billings in these situations to make up for the extra time, and this is a good strategy. Think of it as being paid for on-the-job training.

When It's About the Customer

The customer is not always right, nor does the customer have the right to:

- act abusively toward you;
- ask you to do anything illegal; or
- delay or deny payment without cause.

Just as you are obligated to treat your customers fairly, they should be civil in return. You are under no obligation to maintain a working relationship with a customer who causes you more problems than the income is worth. Don't worry about getting a negative reputation over this. Your good work elsewhere will speak for itself.

The Handyman's Ten Golden Rules

1. Do your jobs as agreed upon with your customers.
2. Charge accordingly for your work.
3. Report all cash and bartering as income.
4. Pay all your suppliers on time.
5. Treat your employees as you would want to be treated if you were an employee.
6. Write and abide by clear and accurate contracts.
7. When billing time and materials, keep an accurate accounting of each.
8. Do not discuss your customers' private lives in any manner that would identify them, unless it's a matter for law enforcement.
9. If the job calls for a permit, get a permit.
10. Dispose of all waste and debris properly.

10 | Marketing Your Business

Handymen are, by definition and title, very hands-on workers. You fix and repair, get bruised, and build calluses, and you can be pretty dirty by the end of the day. Terms like *market share, branding,* and *growing the business* are often just so much blather promoted by marketing people who, you suspect, have never repaired a leaky faucet or have any idea how to flip a tripped circuit breaker on. As you divide the world up into the useful and less-than-useful individuals (in terms of your handyman business), marketing and advertising firms easily end up in the latter category.

Like it or not, though, you'll have to do *some* marketing to get your name out to potential customers. You have many avenues available to you, from a cardboard sign in your truck window to a sixty-second spot during the Super Bowl. The main points to remember when marketing your business are:

- Figure out who your customers are and aim your efforts at them. Sure, you can say everyone is a potential customer, but some—property managers, retired couples, or new parents—are more likely targets for your focus.
- Once you identify a group, keep your name out in front of them on a regular basis.
- Don't spread your marketing money too thin. Paying a skywriter probably won't be as good a use of your budget as business cards.

Marketing doesn't have to absorb a lot of your time or budget. As your business grows and your name gets out there, you could conceivably cut back on your advertising.

People Are Talking about You

The least-expensive marketing is word of mouth. It's also the most difficult to measure because you never know when or if you'll be mentioned to a potential customer. Some contractors swear by it, claiming that once they do a few jobs, the word spreads and they're so busy they never get a break. However, you might want to hedge your bets and spread the word a bit further.

Way back in the days when there were just telephones and homemaker moms chatting with the neighbors, such mentions were made by one person, or perhaps a small group, at a time. Then the Internet showed up and changed everything.

Now, with social networks and blogs, your name can get out within days to more people than you could ever possibly work for. This is great if positive things are said about you, and less than great if someone is badmouthing you—with or without good reason. The main social networks that can apply to you are:

- www.MySpace.com
- www.Facebook.com
- www.LinkedIn.com
- www.Yelp.com
- www.Classmates.com

There are also many lesser-known, more-specialized networks which will show up on an Internet search for "social networks." MySpace and Facebook are general sites where users post their profiles for free and then snoop around, looking for their friends or possible new friends. If anyone finds a handyman that they like and have had an exceptional experience with, they will probably mention them.

All A-Twitter

Twitter (www.twitter.com), a more-recent social networking site, could prove to be increasingly useful as it develops beyond its current short text-based postings.

LinkedIn.com offers professionals an opportunity to meet each other digitally. As their Web site states, "LinkedIn is an interconnected network of experienced professionals from around the world, representing 170 industries and 200 countries. You can find, be introduced to, and collaborate with qualified professionals that you need to work with to accomplish your goals."

Yelp.com features consumer reviews of businesses. It's been in the news lately, as some disgruntled business owners have registered lawsuits against negative reviewers. As Yelp grows and covers more cities, you could find your business being reviewed. It's advisable to check this site from time to time to read what, if anything, is being written about you.

Classmates.com lists former classmates who have registered with the site. It's a good way to let your friends know that you've opened a new business, and the services you offer.

All of these sites can be used to your advantage. Visit each one and consider registering, free of charge. Write a compelling and accurate description of yourself and the business—you don't have to reveal any more personal information than you're comfortable with, although some people reveal *way* too much. As people read about you or spread the word, the information spreads to other sites, thus giving you more contacts and potential customers. And who knows—you might find romance as well.

SOCIAL NETWORKS
PROFESSIONAL NETWORKS
RANDOM FRIENDS
CURRENT USERS (SPRING 2009)

Facebook.com	55 million (American), over 100 million worldwide
MySpace.com	75 million (American), over 100 million worldwide)
Classmates.com	Over 40 million
LinkedIn.com	Over 35 million
Yelp.com	Over 20 million

Blogs

A blog is an online diary, commentary, musings, or your babbling to the world at large. Some are quite popular and interactive with readers who send in questions and responses to blogged information. A blog must be kept current to maintain its readership. If you've got the time to do handyman work and maintain a handyman blog, that's great, but don't sacrifice your jobs for your blog.

Leaving Your Mark

To help ensure follow-up when a customer mentions your name to a friend or relative, be sure to leave extra business cards and flyers at the end of a job. Also, ask if you can use this customer as a reference.

Crank Up the Printer

Digital age or not, we still use and read printed paper. For your handyman business purposes, you have to decide the best advertising venues to get the most bang for your buck.

Your print ads can be displayed in:

- Local and neighborhood newspapers
- Bulletins at places of worship (church, synagogue, mosque)
- Monthly regional magazines
- Your own newsletter

Major local papers have expensive advertising rates, and with decreasing readership and shrinking classified sections, there's little point in advertising a handyman business in them. Weekly papers are a better bet, but check the rates and look at ads similar to the one you would be placing. Call up a few of the painters and other tradespeople that advertise and, if they're willing to talk about it, ask if they get much response from their ads. Weekly papers have much livelier classified sections than major daily papers. Unless there's a specific handyman or odd jobs section, you will have to run multiple ads under painting, carpentry, and so on. If so, ask for a discount rate on your ads.

If you attend religious services, an ad in the weekly bulletin isn't a bad idea. They're usually inexpensive, and this shows support for your place of worship. Regional magazines are often glossy, slick, and aimed at higher-income earners. These people can afford your services. Check out other advertisers to see if they mention other blue-collar trades such as yours; if not, there's probably a good reason for their absence, and you'll want to carefully consider advertising here. One argument says you'll stand out because you'll be the sole advertiser of your type, and another says no one will be looking for or notice a handyman among the jewelry-store and restaurant ads.

Writing and distributing a monthly newsletter takes some effort, depending on how effusive you want to be in your writing. While this can easily be distributed electronically, you should also arrange to leave copies at your local hardware or lumber stores.

Flyers, Brochures, and Door Hangers

As mentioned earlier, you will need a supply of flyers and brochures outlining your services, special offers, pricing, and contact information. The most effective of the three to leave at a home is probably the door hanger, as there's more of a tendency to read this odd-shaped advertisement that you have to physically remove from a doorknob, as opposed to a flyer stuck in the door or under a doormat. According to recent Internet-advertised prices, door hangers, depending on the number of colors and type of finish, can cost less than a dime each, but minimum orders are a thousand or more for the lowest prices.

Self-Promotion

Order some plastic yard signs and place them outside every job you're working on. Attach a business card holder on the signpost as well.

Customer Targets

Not everyone can afford your services. Others who can easily afford them won't use you because they either prefer doing their own work or want to save money. Obviously, you want your marketing efforts to target those who are most likely to hire you. These would include:

- Upper-level-income earners with more money than time to do their own repairs
- Property managers
- Real estate agents and brokers
- Insurance companies
- Condominium associations
- Home inspectors
- Banks with an inventory of foreclosed homes
- Home warranty companies
- Local historical preservation society
- Nonprofit housing groups

- Handicapped and disabled
- Sellers of disassembled furniture needing at-home assembly
- Funeral homes and cemetery directors

In my experience, upper-income earners would rather be earning upper incomes than repairing stuff around the house, although the exceptions, according to my very unscientific observations, seem to be physicians and engineers. Lawyers, accountants, and tech managers—and others whose business involves money, typing away at keyboards, and attending a lot of meetings—can and will use you.

Direct Mail

How do you make yourself known to these potential customers? Consider direct mailing. The Yellow Pages will list all the legal, medical, and accounting firms in your area. You can cross-reference the names and find individual home addresses using the White Pages, and send your compelling, eyeball-grabbing flyer or other announcement there, not to office addresses where it will get tossed out.

No More Licking

Want to simplify your mailing? Go to www.stamps.com and download official USPS postage to your envelopes or packages.

This is where creativity is critical: You really need to stand out among all the excessive mail and advertising we all receive (and throw away with barely a glance) every day. Each flyer or announcement can have the same text on one side, identifying you and your services, and on the other side, a message targeted at a specific occupation. For instance:

- Use a photo—humorous, historic, or contemporary—of a physician or medical procedure with some accompanying text: "All day long, it's blood, guts, and hospital gowns. Do you really want to fix a faucet when you get home?"
- For attorneys and judges, try a Victorian-era courtroom drawing with the caption, "You're looking for order in the court. We'll bring order to your home."

- A line of coffee cups, followed by, "Haven't you had enough stimulation for one day?" (aimed at managers, tech workers, and similarly employed).

The possibilities are endless, but be aware of the printing and mailing costs. Currently, it costs 28 cents to mail a 6-by-4.25-inch postcard, and 44 cents for larger postcards. Bulk mailing rates really apply to large mailings and require a special permit (see http://pe.usps.com/businessmail101/welcome.htm).

You can also direct-mail an all-purpose card or announcement to certain zip codes.

Where do you find zip-code-based addresses, let alone the names of the residents? You can use a bulk mailing service, which will:

- provide a variety of printed materials for mailing postcards, brochures, letters, and flyers;
- blanket large areas;
- find very exacting demographic groups by income, age, marital status, and how long they've lived in their home; and
- probably require multiple mailings.

Or, you can spend some time at the library and snoop through the Cole Information Services directory (www.coleinformation.com), which cross-references names and addresses in cities all over the country. These directories are expensive, and your library will probably only have one copy, which, as a reference manual, cannot be checked out, so keep this in mind when you plan your research.

Not All Are Free

Be sure you have permission to reproduce any photos or images you grab off the Internet to use in your marketing materials. Some are free, while others are fee-based.

Property Managers

Property managers will either have an in-house maintenance staff or will hire out contractors as needed to take care of repairs on rental properties. Some managers handle multiple buildings, and others live in the building or complex they manage. These are good people to know because they always have something needing fixing, especially the larger properties. An Internet search, or even looking in the Yellow Pages for your area, will bring up a good sampling of local managers for you to contact. You can find local apartment and property managers by doing a search on "apartment associations (your city)." Most will have a members' magazine available that features managers' advertisements.

Once you've established yourself with a property manager, inquire about setting up a maintenance contract: You show up monthly for a set hourly rate, vs. a rate per type of job. This can be very steady money and good filler work if you find yourself with a hole in your schedule. Contact commercial property owners as well. They may require your services when a retail or office tenant moves out, and they can also recommend you to those they lease space to, for their own in-house repairs.

Real Estate Agents and Brokers

Some realty firms also do property management. Otherwise, they can be a source of both direct jobs and referrals to clients who have purchased properties, or are trying to sell and need some work done prior to listing. Expect a variety of tasks, such as gutter cleaning, dripping faucets, and perhaps some general clean-up and hauling. Even new homes call for alterations, such as:

- Changing out fixtures
- Installing shelving and other storage units
- Changing paint colors
- Installing additional locks

In areas of multiple new homes, you could end up with a lot of business.

Another market is vacation properties and second homes, which might be managed through local real estate companies.

Insurance Companies

Whether it's storm damage or the result of vandalism, homeowners' insurance covers a lot of repairs, many of them too small for a general contractor. Local insurance companies need reliable handymen to handle this work promptly, which will include door and window repair, fire damage–related projects, and fixing leaks.

Condominium Associations

Condominiums undergo both large-scale scheduled projects, such as exterior and common-area painting, and everyday smaller repairs. Both an association and individual owners need dependable contractors for these repairs, and can be a source of steady work. If you pursue these clients, try and schedule as many customers as possible on the same day to cut down on your travel time.

Targeted Strike

If a condo association isn't interested in your services, target individual condo owners. You wouldn't need specific owners' names for a direct mailing, just the address and unit numbers.

Home Inspectors

Home inspectors, by the very nature of their work, find problems when they inspect a house. Some must be repaired before a home can be sold, or are discovered after purchase and need to be addressed. It's a conflict of interest for a home inspector to do the repairs, but a list of preferred service providers, including handymen, can be provided to homeowners.

Bank Foreclosures

Home foreclosures are a fact of life, and have become much more prominent recently due to unregulated loans and mortgage brokers and buyers behaving badly. These homes often need to be secured, cleaned out, their yards at least minimally maintained, and need repairs due to vandalism. At the time of this writing, some of the most successful businesses associated with the crashing real estate market are those that board up windows and replace locks on abandoned, foreclosed houses. The size of this market will shrink, but there will always be some foreclosed properties needing work. Start with your own bank's mortgage officers and introduce your services. They will no doubt have the names of fellow bankers you can talk to as well.

> **It Pays to Be Careful**
>
> Foreclosed homes sometimes have people living in them illegally as squatters. Some are homeless, some are criminals, but none are legitimate residents. Even if you've been assured that the homes are vacant, use caution when entering.

Home Warranty Companies

New homes typically come with a builder's warranty. Any problems arising within the first year are taken care of by the builder or an appropriate subcontractor. Some homeowners purchase a separate extended warranty from a warranty corporation. As these corporations are not necessarily locally based, they need local contractors to perform warranty repairs. Do a search on "home warranty coverage" and contact any companies that offer policies in your area.

Historical Preservation Groups

Most cities and towns have historic homes, along with homes that are simply older, and trying to be historic. The local preservation societies are often looking for funds to purchase and renovate these places, and they tend to have limited budgets. Nevertheless, the properties under their care need winterizing, glass repair, holes patched to keep pigeons out, and minor roof repairs, until full restoration can be done at a later date. Other buildings have been renovated and rented out, but need maintenance from time to time.

This is where you step in, especially if you have some restoration credentials and can talk the talk about repairing old double-hung windows or replacing missing wainscoting. I wouldn't expect there would be a lot of work from preservation groups, and you might more often be roped into donating some free repairs (not a bad idea from time to time), but contact them anyway. The more people who know about you, the better off you will be.

Nonprofit Housing

Many localities have nonprofit housing, built and/or administered by local agencies. In larger metropolitan areas, thousands of units of low- and moderate-income housing exist and need maintenance. These properties include renovated historic structures and new residential and commercial construction. It's likely the managing agency has a maintenance staff, but they could be looking for backup or supplemental help when the workload is unusually large.

New Market Possibilities

Consider marketing to day-care centers and preschools, many of whom have single-parent families. You can even consider a discount for single-parent households who, fair or not, are typically run by mothers. And mothers are generally less exposed than fathers to home repairs and tools growing up. You could both fill a need and enter a solid market.

Handicapped and Disabled

Housing for the disabled is often subsidized, and referred or provided by nonprofit housing groups. Another side to this market, however, is the need to make adjustments inside existing homes for those finding themselves newly disabled or in need of assistance due to an accident, medical operation, or aging. These adjustments can include:

- Building wheelchair ramps
- Lowering doorknobs
- Installing bathroom grab bars
- Widening doorways and adjusting cabinets/counters for wheelchair mobility

Some alterations might be reimbursed by health-care insurance. By introducing yourself to physical and occupational therapists, particularly those who do home visits, you could find a regular source of referrals.

U-Assemble Furniture

Ikea, Crate and Barrel, Sauder, and other manufacturers sell extensive lines of ready-to-assemble (RTA) and flat-pack furniture. Naturally, professional furniture assemblers have established themselves to assist the frustrated and less-than-cheery buyers, and you can do the same. If you are experienced in furniture assembly, this is a good niche to consider, especially in large urban areas with a lot of apartments, as these are big markets for these manufacturers.

The other side of this furniture coin is the market for *disassembling* already-built furniture so it can be moved in and out of tight spaces in residences. Dr. Sofa (www .drsofa.com) in New York City disassembles upholstered sofas and such and reassembles them after they've been moved to their final destination. This is clearly a very specialized service, but it can extend to wall storage units and beds as well (which, unlike sofas, require no reupholstering).

Finishing the Unfinished

Another market to consider is finishing unfinished wood furniture after purchase. Some customers have the best intentions to stain and finish their new raw dining room table, but when it doesn't happen, you can step in.

Gravesite Maintenance

Although it sounds a bit morbid, gravesite maintenance has its share of practitioners who clean headstones, cut and trim grass, and generally tidy up the sites.

This is a service that is especially helpful to out-of-state family members, as well as those who are elderly or live far from the burial site and cannot perform the routine upkeep to their satisfaction. Do a search on "gravesite maintenance" to get further information on what this work entails. Once you feel comfortable offering this service, introduce yourself to area funeral homes and cemetery directors for referrals, bearing in mind that they might offer this service themselves and thus view you as a competitor. Smaller, more off-the-beaten-path graveyards might have more potential for clients.

Special and Seasonal Promotions

Painters routinely offer spring specials—"Book now for summer exterior painting and get a discounted price." You can do the same thing, only you can offer it for any job; say, 10 percent off your normal rates if booked during the winter months, when work might be slow (although if you live in a snow belt, offer to plow driveways and sidewalks to stay busy).

Every season brings certain maintenance needs and the opportunity for special services.

Winter

- Snow removal
- Hang outdoor holiday lights
- Clean, touch up paint/stain, and repair all outdoor furniture and place in storage
- Drain sprinkler system

Spring

- Remove storm windows, install screens
- Repair winter roof damage
- Check gutters for loose areas and debris
- Patch newly cracked driveways and walkways
- Prepare garden for planting

Summer

- Exterior and interior painting

- Yard work of all types
- Deck and siding repairs
- Window repairs

Fall

- Insulate pipes
- Chop firewood
- Clean gutters
- Install weather stripping

You can offer package deals with a list of services and a flat rate for the typical home—and all the better if you can establish regular maintenance contracts with homeowners. This is predictable income, for the most part; it keeps you busy, and allows you some control over your scheduling.

Preferred Installer Status

Some companies qualify and/or train contractors who install their products. Mr. Grab Bar (www.mrgrabbar.com) is one of them. Armstrong, the flooring manufacturer (www.armstrong.com) is another. Home Depot designates qualified contractors as Professional Installation Service Providers. While some may doubt the value of these programs, they're worth considering, as they can boost your business through professional referrals and also provide you with more credibility. Check with every company whose products you use and see if they offer training, certificates, or other qualifying credentials. See chapter 12 for more information.

Charitable Work

Undoubtedly, you could volunteer your services every day of the year and never exhaust all the possible charitable and nonprofit avenues for needed handyman work. There's no need to go overboard, but occasional volunteer work, especially of the high-profile variety, can both do the recipient and your business some good.

- Such work will result in new contacts.
- You could get mentioned in the local newspaper or on the news if the project is reported.
- You'll meet other contractors who can become referral sources.

Choose your projects thoughtfully. You want work that's clearly defined, a work-site that's ready for you, and a competent project manager. Even if the common notion of charity work is to be as selflessly motivated as possible, you might as well pick something you're good at, where your work will shine.

And bring some business cards to pass out.

Press Releases

Write press releases for your local and neighborhood newspapers for any unusual work you do as a charitable contribution (repairing local homes for lower-income owners, for instance). Press releases only cost you a little time, and there's always a chance you'll get some publicity out of them.

Internet Marketing

The aforementioned social networking sites are one way to use the Internet, but they are indirect advertising. A more direct approach requires:

- Your own Web site
- Linking with and from complementary Web sites
- Possibly placing some small advertisements

Internet use and marketing will be covered in chapter 11.

Marketing a Niche Service

Specialty services that most people can use on occasion but cannot find contractors to do will give you an advantage over other handymen. Maybe you're expert at transplanting full-grown shrubs without damaging them, or you excel in screen repair. Weather-stripping—particularly if you can install metal weather stripping—is an uncommon talent. Others include:

- Locating and eliminating floor squeaks, especially when they're under carpet
- Tile and countertop repairs

- Wood window restoration
- Plaster and stucco work
- On-site furniture repair
- Anything with the word "green" in it (i.e., eco-friendly)

You might find yourself doing mostly niche work once you develop a reputation for it—and they could be the repairs you like to do the least! Nevertheless, they can be very profitable and predictable. Review your skills and determine which you want to heavily emphasize in your marketing.

A Card for Every Purpose

There's no reason why you can't have two sets of business cards—one as a general handyman and one emphasizing a specialty skill.

Press Release

A press release is an announcement, written in third person, and designed to pique the interest of an editor or reporter. You want them to believe that whatever is being announced is newsworthy and deserves attention from the news media. A press release by its nature is biased toward the announcement itself. On page 170 is one format for a press release.

Everyone Likes a Freebie

I recall a *Wall Street Journal* article discussing which hotel guests especially like to take home the small soaps and bottles of shampoo, conditioner, and lotion from their hotel rooms: It was the well-to-do. No one needed them, and some gave bags of their collected toiletries to homeless shelters, but they took them nevertheless. Most of us like free stuff, whether we have any use for it or not.

Your free stuff will be wanted, too. You have to decide if giving away baubles, balloons, notepads, or pens with your company name on them is a good use of your marketing dollars. Trade-show booth sponsors give away free "swag" all the time,

COMPANY LOGO

Contact: (Your Name)
Phone
FOR IMMEDIATE RELEASE
E-mail

MAIN TITLE OF PRESS RELEASE (ALL CAPITAL LETTERS AND BOLD)

First paragraph: Who, what, when, where, and why. List your city and state, the date of the press release, and a brief summary ("Merlin's Magic Home Care announces free repair and maintenance classes for first-time home buyers at the Camelot Neighborhood Center . . .").

Following paragraphs: Fill out the details and tell something about your work, including how long you've been in business and the types of repairs you do.

Last paragraph: "For additional information, please contact . . ."

but only a marketing company will tell you that this necessarily leads to more sales. From my limited experience, it seems to lead to show attendees, including other vendors, grabbing and collecting the swag simply because they can. Do an Internet search on "promotional products" and see what's available. Then, think of a venue where giving a promotional product away while introducing yourself to potential new customers would make good sense. For instance, you can meet product vendors at a local home improvement show, or you can meet fellow parents at a sporting event for your children.

It's one thing to mindlessly hand out key chains or letter openers with your company information on them and another to give them out after you've introduced yourself and made a personal connection, albeit a brief one.

Radio and TV

Commuters are captive listeners for radio stations, although the ability to readily change stations or pop in a CD means listener loyalty is a bit fickle. The cost of a radio ad varies according to the:

- popularity of the radio station and its subsequent market share;
- ratings of the particular shows you consider for your advertising;
- how frequently your ads are played; and
- TSL (time spent listening).

In addition, you will have production costs, which you'll most likely handle through a professional firm. This is a very pricey way to market a small handyman company. Consider it down the line when you're running fifty crews from your beachfront home in Hawaii.

Community Access Television (CAT)

Does your area have community access television? CAT accepts proposals for new shows, and one of those shows could be yours. Whether a handyman show televised at two in the morning will bring you any customers remains to be seen, but if you're a frustrated thespian who can create enough screen presence to gain an unexpected audience share, who knows? Fees for use of production facilities will vary depending on the station, but as a rule they are very modest, and often include some training sessions.

Home Shows

The fees for booth space at home improvement shows vary depending on the size of the show and the size and location of the booth. I would be reluctant to recommend that a one- or two-person business put out this kind of expenditure (including constructing a display) during the first year or so in business. However, going to these shows and introducing yourself to vendors, bankers, real estate agents, and others, being sure to bring a lot of brochures and business cards with you, is a quick and inexpensive way to spread the word about your handyman business to a lot of people at one time.

Stretching Your Marketing Dollars

Like most small contracting businesses, it may be difficult for you to establish a marketing budget. You're all dressed up and ready to go, but without advertising or spreading the word about yourself, you're all alone without a prom date. Personal contacts—via the Internet, phone, or shoe leather—will take time, but will bring the most return initially without costing any money out of pocket. Why? When we associate a person with a business, we are more inclined to remember both, at least if the experience in meeting the owner—that's you—is a positive one.

It's easy to overspend on printed materials and print ads, so stick with the person-to-person approach at the start. In addition:

- *Be sure your vehicle has a sign that's as eye-catching as you can afford!* It's free advertising every time you park it, whether you're on a job or out for a night on the town.
- Printed T-shirts with the company name and phone number turn everyone wearing one into a walking advertisement. (If family members or friends wear them, give them business cards to pass out as well.)

- Carefully weigh placing an ad in paper versions of the Yellow Pages. As mentioned in chapter 4, there are regional and local versions available, thus making it difficult to decide which one is best. It's also debatable whether upcoming generations will even use them. You can spend your money better elsewhere.

Learn to Blow Your Horn!

Are you an introvert, uncomfortable with cold-calling or dropping in on hardware and lumber stores to promote your new business? Just because you're a handyman doesn't mean you can do everything well, so consider hiring this out. We all know natural-born salespeople who grab and hold our attention—everyone else's, too.

Even if you loathe marketing, think of it as a chance to toot your own horn and become known to potential customers. You can put the horn away as you get more successful, because your work will speak for you.

Choose Your Advertising Medium Wisely

Not all marketing efforts produce the same results per dollar spent. According to one 2006 study (note the word "one"), "The New eCommerce Decade: The Age of Micro Targeting" by Piper Jaffray & Company, the average cost to a business for one new customer via the Internet was $8.50, but it cost $20 to gain a customer from Yellow Pages advertising, $60 from e-mail, and $70 from direct mail. A handyman is a specialized service, and you won't be sending out tens of thousands of mailers to potential customers, so these numbers are not entirely pertinent to you—other than to show which advertising medium in general pays off the best for mass advertisers.

Marketing Strategies by Cost

FREE

- Social Web sites
- MySpace.com
- Facebook.com
- In-person introductions to promote your business
- Property managers
- Real estate agents
- Nonprofit housing groups
- Senior centers

LOW COST

- Brochures
- Flyers
- Newsletter

MODERATE COST

- Direct mailing
- Ads in bulletins at places of worship

HIGHER COST

- Discounts and seasonal specials
- Your own company Web site
- Promotional gifts

HIGHEST COST

- Ongoing Yellow Pages ad
- Regular ad in major newspaper
- Radio ad

The Internet and E-Commerce

The Internet, it seems, has combined television, paper mail, newspapers, and the telephone system in one grand combo pack. Information and every degree of exposure are a few mouse clicks away. If you're not using it, your kids are, and so are many potential customers. You can market your business several ways via the Internet:

- Build your own Web site.
- Participate in home-repair forums.
- Post repair and maintenance articles on your Web site, and others.
- Use e-mail creatively and regularly.
- You can purchase advertising on relevant sites.

Since you're selling a service and not a physical product, you could conceivably receive an overwhelming response to a Web presence and end up with a massive job backlog. There are certainly *worse* problems for a small business to encounter.

Your Web Site

As discussed in chapter 6, you can build your own Web site or contract it out. In the early days of the Internet, building a site meant writing your own HTML code, developing your own designs, and loading your own images. It also meant high hourly fees for Web designers. Now, templates are available that you can click and load without doing any coding. The result will not be the most sophisticated of sites, but it will be more than acceptable for your purposes.

Feeling more adventurous? Prefer buying some Web design software? This is not an inexpensive route to go, and easily more than you need, but take a look at:

- Microsoft Expression Web 2 ($299, www.microsoft.com/expression/products/purchase.aspx?key=Web)
- Adobe Dreamweaver CS4 ($399, www.adobe.com/products/dreamweaver/)

You can find less-expensive alternatives including various freeware programs by searching "Web site design templates," but do you really want to go to all this trouble? Web hosting services offer easy-to-build templates and design services, along with hosting and maintaining your site. (You'll have to use one of these unless you have your own Web server, in which case you're likely rolling in money and have little reason to become a handyman other than for your own amusement.) They exist to make your life easier (and to earn income for themselves, naturally).

Oddly enough, a Web search as of this writing does not come up with many individual handyman sites. There are sites for the national franchises and how to be your own handyman around the house, but it seems few individual businesses are up and running on the Web. Granted, this was not an exhaustive search, and regional searches will reveal more, but the field seems wide open for new handyman Web sites.

Getting on the Web

Want to establish a really quick Web presence? Go to www.squidoo.com and fill in a few blanks and you'll have a finished page. According to their site, "Squidoo is a hand-built collection of nearly 900,000 pages built by people just like you." The pages have advertisements covering about a third of the usable space, but if you just want to get some info out about your company, the price is right.

What to Include

Your Web site can be as extensive or as restrained as you wish. Once you've introduced yourself, explained your services, and provided contact information, you can call it good, or fill in the additional page space. Photos of your work—in before-and-after format—are especially illuminating for potential customers; however, they can eat up space depending on how large a site you contract for with your Web host (see next section). You can also include a photo of yourself:

- standing by your vehicle with your company name on the side;
- surrounded by all your tools, laid out in an appealing design;
- working a job; or simply
- a clear head shot.

Many Web pages are far too crowded with text and images, making them hard to read. *You don't have to fill every square inch—leave some white space!*

Sample Web Site

For one example of a handyman's Web site, go to www.naturalhandyman.com.

Links

The more sites you're linked to, the better! This means increased traffic for your own Web site. You can be directly linked from another site, or be linked in an article or write-up about your company. Some sites will ask you to reciprocate and link to them, which is a fair exchange.

Some ways to build up your links include:

- Create some easy-to-remember docs, such as "101 Maintenance Tips" or "Top 10 Handyman Mistakes."
- Submit your site to www.dmoz.org, which is a free Web directory.
- Answer questions at http://answers.yahoo.com/ or http://groups.google .com/.
- If you or a friend has the know-how, build an interactive tool, such as a deck calculator that determines the amount of materials needed to build a deck (a Web search on "deck calculators" will show some examples).

There are many articles and strategies, as well as link-building firms, accessible on the Internet (search under "linking strategies"), but it can be overkill for a small handyman business. You'll get plenty of responses just for having the word *handyman* in your title, and I do recommend this, or something similar ("handyman services" or "handyman jobs," for instance). Web searches are affected by keywords, and *handyman* will get you plenty of attention.

Web Hosting

A Web host is a business that provides server space for Web sites. A server—or, more accurately, a bank of servers—is a computer that stores your Web pages along with those of other customers. A server is accessed every time someone clicks on a Web site. Your chosen Web host will maintain your files and offer other Web services that relate to your site, such as site design and domain (your site's name) registration.

There are a *lot* of Web hosting services, from Yahoo to Bluehost, mentioned earlier. Do a search on "Web host services" and names will show up that you've never heard of, all of varying reliability and price. There are even free hosting services, but they come with limitations.

What should you look for in a Web host?

- Managed, dedicated service
- True 24/7 support
- Number of years in business

There is no perfect hosting service. Do an Internet search on "best hosting services" and *every* site that comes up with a survey has different winners and losers (and every site suggests it is the *only* site to make these determinations). A little research will narrow down the top two or three contenders for your business, but keep in mind that your site will be fairly simple. You're strictly offering information and not a lot of interactivity, so don't take what every reviewer geek complains about too much to heart. As long as the service is stable, with little or no downtime problems, the site-building templates are easy to use, and there aren't a lot of complaints about the costs or hidden fees, you should be fine.

There's No Such Thing as a Free Lunch

There are some free hosting services, but your site will be limited in size and will feature advertisements unrelated to your business. The largest and best known of these services is Yahoo's GeoCities (http://geocities.yahoo.com/). The advertisements, banners, and pop-ups pay for the free hosting. Reliability with the smaller free hosting services can always be an issue, but if you're on a really limited budget and just want to experiment with a Web site, take a closer look at GeoCities.

Domain Name

Your Web site's domain name—the part that comes after "www." and before ".com" or ".net"—can be your business name or whatever else you choose. Your business name is the most logical, however, and will more likely attract your current customers if they search for you on the Web. When you sign up with a hosting service, they will, for a fee, do a domain search to confirm that your chosen name isn't already in use, and they will also register your domain name.

Dynamic Site or Snoozer?

Your Web site doesn't have to change as often as former headliner rock 'n' rollers announce their retirement tours (and then annoyingly keep coming back year after year), but the content should be refreshed periodically to maintain reader interest. Tim Carter's "Ask the Builder" (www.askthebuilder.com) site, for instance, adds new information regularly, while maintaining an archive of past articles and answers to reader questions.

If you can become a respected source of information, you can package and sell anything from painting instructions to a collection of your special tricks in simple brochures. Tim Carter sells checklists, e.g., *Exterior Painting & Staining Checklist*, for $17 each! How complicated can it be to make up a checklist, even a thorough one? If you do sell anything on your Web site, you'll have to be set up to take credit card payments either directly, if you have an Internet merchant account (a little much unless you have a lot of sales), or through a service such as ProPay (www.propay.com) or PayPal (www.paypal.com).

Keep in mind that if you decide to sell something out of your shop—birdhouses, cutting boards, recycled window and door hardware that you've restored—you will need to get set up for packaging and shipping. Printed material can be sent out via e-mail in PDF format, which keeps the file sizes manageable and easy to send.

User-generated e-mail should be answered weekly at the very least. You will want to stay up on the latest and greatest materials and methodologies for home repair. You don't have to know everything, of course, but enough to keep your readers coming back.

> ### Getting Reader Feedback through Your Web Site
>
> Use your Web site to learn from your readers. Periodically, I receive letters from readers of my window repair book (*Working Windows: A Guide to the Repair and Restoration of Wood Windows*, Lyons Press), or one of the maintenance columns I write for several California-based apartment owner magazines. They point out something I didn't know or could do differently, which is great for me, as I can use the information later should a situation call for it.

Speaking of E-Mail

As you build your customer base and perhaps answer questions from your Web site readers, you'll also be building an e-mail list. Sending excessive messages to this e-mail list is a sure way to annoy the recipients, but you can send:

- A monthly newsletter
- Reminders of seasonal maintenance
- Announcements of new services
- Discount coupons for e-mail users only

You might maintain a consistent subject line, such as A NOTE FROM ROCKY'S HANDYMAN SERVICES, so that there will be less chance of your recipients deleting it as junk mail.

Use a professional signature to close all of your e-mail correspondence. The signature should include:

- Your name
- The name of your company
- Company logo
- Business address and phone number

E-mail programs will create this signature and include it with all of your correspondence. You might consider a custom background—but not one that's too distracting—for your e-mail as well. The background should not be too busy or dark in color.

Forums

Do a search on home-repair forums and you'll find plenty of sites full of musings, plaintive queries, and expert and not-so-expert responses. These are good places to see what kinds of problems homeowners are facing, the types of solutions available, and what other handymen are thinking, as they and other small contractors are regular contributors to these forums. These forums are both national and local (e.g., the Berkeley Parents Network, http://parents.berkeley.edu/, which is local but with a more widespread readership), so your participation will not automatically lead to any contacts with local homeowners, but there's every reason to believe it could.

Keep your comments positive, accurate, and clear. Write them off-line first, proofreading carefully for spelling, grammar, and punctuation before posting.

What Is an Avatar Anyway?

Consider using an avatar when you answer questions in a forum. An avatar is a graphic, often somewhat whimsical representation of you, using a photo, video clip, or drawing. You can create one at www.faceyourmanga.com/welcome.htm, or at any number of other avatar sites by searching for "free avatar."

Craigslist

Craigslist (www.craigslist.com) is in an Internet league by itself. The mostly free posting service (they charge for job postings) gets over twelve *billion* page views per month. You can list your business under "services/skilled trade" in any of over 550 cities worldwide. *Everyone* uses craigslist, and some observers believe it is steadily replacing many newspaper classified ads.

You'll have to renew your craigslist posting regularly. As new ads get posted (and they post very quickly), your ad will get knocked down the list, making it less likely to be seen. Consider creating a couple of different ads and posting both of them a few days apart—but don't post over and over again. Craigslist users do not hesitate to flame anyone they think is abusing the posting service.

Visuals are a big plus on craigslist! Use photos and appropriate graphics in your ads. Look at a sampling of ads under the "creative" link, as these tend to be more visually appealing and less purely functional than skilled-trade ads.

Paying for Internet Advertising

In addition to social networking sites, e-mailing, and craigslist.com, paid advertising is also available on the Internet. An online agency will, for a fee:

- list your site with major search engines (Google, Yahoo, etc.) for maximum optimization;
- develop and place classified ads on multiple Web sites; and
- offer programs such as Cost per Visitor (CPV) or Cost per Click (CPC), whereby you are charged for every visitor delivered to your Web site, or every time someone clicks on a link to your site.

The fees vary depending on what level of service you purchase. You can do some of this yourself by using Google AdWords (http://adwords.google.com/), mentioned earlier.

Is this overkill for a sole proprietor handyman business? Probably; but if your budget allows for some experimentation, say one or two months' worth of paid advertising, what can it hurt (other than your bank balance)? For more information, do a search on "Internet advertising."

Creating a business Web site

- Build it yourself
- Proprietary software
- Free software
- Need to learn design basics, key search words
- Build with a Web host template
- Fill-in-the-blanks approach
- Design limitations, but much easier for those without site-building knowledge
- Up and running same day

Hosting a Web site

- Web hosting service for a fee
- Prices and services vary
- Very affordable, particularly for small sites
- Offer domain-name search and registration
- Free Web hosting
- Limitations include tech support and inclusion of ads
- Geocities.com is best-known free hosting site

Maintaining a Web site

- As the owner, you should regularly update the site and answer all e-mails

Forums

- Free participation, registration often required to post question or comment
- You can get Web exposure for your expertise

Blog

- Requires a Web site
- Post on subjects of interest to you and potential customers
- Blogs include strictly personal and/or professional information

Craigslist

- Free posting for your business
- Good site for finding used tools and materials

Paying for ads

- Google is most likely site for ads; check their rates

12 | Training and Certification

There have always been innovations in product lines and tools, but never before has there been such a range of finishes, adhesives, fasteners, power tools, and other sundry home-repair and maintenance necessities as are available today. Some new products are not used in the same way, or they do not install the way earlier versions did, so you must learn how to use them to achieve the proper results. Although your dealers and suppliers can provide you with information, the more you know the better. Consider paints and finishes; manufacturers are always coming out with new lines. A brief overview of paint types includes:

- Latex, shellac, and spirit-based finishes
- Epoxies, urethanes, cement paints, and chlorinated rubber paints
- Flat, satin, eggshell, semigloss, high gloss, and crackle-finish products
- Primers, sanding sealers, undercoats, and etching materials

Within each of those product categories are dozens of major manufacturers and products. It isn't enough for you to stick with Glidden or Dutch Boy or Benjamin Moore products because you like them, or you've had "good luck" with them in the past. You need to know which finishes within specific product lines are best for the jobs you do. You need to continually educate yourself, and the most immediate resources are found online.

Online Info

For the price of signing on with an Internet service provider (ISP), or some regular trips to your local library's public computers, you can go online and find more repair and maintenance information than you ever dreamed existed. Like everything else in cyberspace, the quality of the information varies from one provider to the next, so read everything with a skeptical eye. Simply do a search on "home repairs" or "do it yourself," and you'll find columnists, blogs, professionals in the field, and amateurs answering every type of repair question.

Product manufacturers and trade groups get in on this virtual free-for-all as well. Go to any paint company's Web site (www.sherwinwilliams.com is a good one), for example, or the National Paint and Coatings Association (www.paint.org), and you'll discover plenty of information on the latest finishes, as well as application techniques and how to solve common painting problems.

Beyond the world of paint, you can also get information on:

- Caulk and sealants (www.dap.com)
- Personal safety equipment (www.3m.com, for printed material and online videos)
- Tools and projects using tools (www.blackanddecker.com)
- Hand tools (www.stanleytools.com)
- Electrical information (www.leviton.com)
- Flooring (www.floorexpert.com)

And the list goes on and on, depending on what you're seeking.

Some Online Tips

When you come across a recommended product, do another search on users' reviews (e.g., "glidden paint review") for some real-world experiences. Keep in mind that some people are never satisfied, and some simply have had bad experiences while so many others have had just the opposite. You'll have to judge for yourself the accuracy of the reviews, but look at a broad sampling.

Another good source of online information is the Web site of any radio or television home-repair series, such as "Hometime" (www.hometime.com), or the sites of print columnists. Online reading and researching is a good way to stay up on new products and ideas, and to learn alternative ways to do jobs.

However, more-thorough course work can provide more-systematic training.

Back to School

Community colleges across the country offer an array of relevant courses for the handyman, including carpentry, plumbing, general construction green building, and business math, to name a few. As a handyman, you can take these classes in order to expand your repertoire of skills or to improve the ones you already have. In addition, these colleges teach:

- Accounting and bookkeeping
- Business law
- Certification programs (e.g., welding, HVAC, or automotive repair)
- General business classes

If you intend on increasing the size of your business to the point where you're doing more managing than field work, business-related classes can speed up your learning curve and in the long run save you money and help you avoid more than a few headaches. You have a choice between community college education and private vocational schools, and I would recommend the former. Why?

- Depending on the classes, community college credits can apply toward a four-year college degree should you choose to continue your education.
- A community college offers more resources.
- When you compare prices and what you get for your money, a community college is often a better deal.

Hands-on Learning

Regardless of where you attend classes, if you have any questions regarding the institution's accreditation, go to www.ed.gov/admins/finaid/accred/index.html, a U.S. Department of Education Web page which links to a list of accredited programs.

Some course work can be done online, but I wouldn't recommend it for any skill that requires hands-on participation. The whole point of taking these classes is to learn from reading, demonstration, and personal involvement, not by sitting alone in front of a computer.

Other Community Resources

If you have a Home Depot or Lowe's home improvement center nearby, you have a source for free, and informal, classroom education. Online how-to video projects are also available, as well as numerous print articles. It's in the best interest of these stores to show customers how to do everything imaginable, and then sell them the materials and tools to complete the projects. You can learn from them, too. Regional home improvement chains are likely to hold their own how-to classes as well.

Depending on where you live—it's more likely to be available in larger cities—the local government might sponsor a housing coalition group which in turn offers various how-to or repair classes. Granted, these are aimed at inexperienced homeowners, but if a class is offered on a topic you're not familiar with, it's worth pursuing. Energy efficiency and green building techniques seem to be popular subjects. For one example, go to www.oaklandpw.com/Page89.aspx (class offerings as of the time of this writing).

Industry Certifications

Various industries offer certification programs for their products. Some are specific to individual companies and others are more applicable to specific categories. For instance, the National Wood Flooring Association offers certifications for:

- Wood flooring installer
- Sander and finisher
- Wood flooring inspector

This might be overkill for a handyman who only does occasional flooring repairs and touch-ups, but floor refinishing could become a profitable sideline, especially for small jobs such as single bedrooms or stairways (refinishing treads and risers is not a favorite activity of flooring companies). Go to www.nwfacp.org for more information.

Handymen deal with doors and windows, both repairing and installing. To become an American Window and Door Institute Certified Installer, look at their program at www.awdi.com/prog.html.

Other available certifications include:

- North American Laminate Flooring Association (www.nalfa.org/retailers InstallerCertificationClass.php)

- Certified Floorcovering Installers (www.cfiinstallers.com)
- Ceramic Tile Education Foundation (www.tileschool.org/)
- Armstrong Certified Installer (www.floorexpert.com/)
- Institute of Inspection, Cleaning, and Restoration (www.iicrc.org/home .shtml)

Is it worth chasing after, and paying for, various certifications? A certification can benefit you if:

- you do enough work with the chosen material that a certification will bring you more credibility with customers;
- the certification program is informative and brings you up-to-date on the newest materials and installation techniques; and
- it allows you to charge more for your services.

Carefully investigate the programs that interest you, as all training is not created equal. Think back to your days in school and remember the teachers that were exceptional—and then those who weren't helpful at all. Contact any local contractors who have taken the training (certified specialists are often listed on the Web sites of those doing the certifying). They might be willing to talk with you about whether it's valuable training, or if you're just collecting a certificate.

Teaching an Option?

Although you won't receive a certificate, local community groups periodically offer home-repair training taught by contractors, some of whom are retired. Many of these classes are entry-level, but they can still have some value. After experiencing one of these classes, you can consider offering to teach a class as well.

Books

There is no end to the number of available home-repair books. Every bookstore is packed with books on plumbing, carpentry, painting, flooring, kitchen renovations, and so on. A huge amount of this material overlaps between the different titles and authors. After all, how many different ways are there to install a faucet washer?

Even an experienced handyman can learn some new tricks, particularly if you pick up a specialty selection such as my book, *Working Windows* (another shameless plug), or tomes on faux painting and finishes. There are some old standards for general repairs (e.g., *Reader's Digest Complete Do-It-Yourself Manual*), as well as very slick and thorough pictorial books (the Black & Decker books stand out in this category).

In addition to perusing bookstores, your public library will have plenty of books to use as resource materials.

Finding Repair Manuals

If you're looking for a source of construction and building-related books, try Builders Booksource (www.buildersbooksource.com), which specializes in trade, building design, and engineering publications.

Repair books show up at garage sales, secondhand stores, and library book sales. They're inexpensive enough to make it worth grabbing anything interesting.

Magazines

Like books, there is a seemingly unending supply of magazines directed to home improvement, interior design, handyman projects, and the like. Magazines pertinent to the handyman business include:

- *The Family Handyman* (naturally)
- *This Old House*
- *Fine Homebuilding*
- *Popular Mechanics*

There are certainly other publications, including ones aimed at specific industries, such as janitorial, window cleaning, painting, etc. although some of these tend to highlight more of the business end rather than techniques and products. A good number of industry Web sites offer free newsletters as well. Do a search on "window cleaning newsletters," "home painting newsletters," and "carpentry repairs newsletter," or search on any other topic of interest and see what shows up. Newsletters written by other contractors tend to be very specific to their businesses and will not offer much repair or educational information. However, they can act as guides for an eventual newsletter of your own.

Historic Preservation Training

Homes and other buildings that are registered landmarks must follow strict guidelines regarding renovations and changes in their appearance. Others are in historic districts and are subject to the rules (some would say whims) of local historical society boards. You cannot, for instance, replace an original wood casement window with a vinyl slider, but you can repair the wood window, or, if it's not repairable, replace it with an identical new sash. Installing aluminum or vinyl siding over nineteenth-century clapboard is a transgression of unspeakable horror. Interiors are often subject to less-stringent regulations (no one expects a homeowner to live with a century-old heating or plumbing system, as quaint as they may sound).

Where do you go for historic preservation training? You could try Columbia University's Preservation Program (www.arch.columbia.edu/hp/), but I can safely say this is way more knowledge than you'll need, unless you want to become a certified conservationist. Closer to home, some states and municipalities offer their own certifications. As an example, the city of Aspen, Colorado, offers a certification program for tradespeople working on historic buildings. The information needed to pass their examination is contained in a city-published training manual (www .aspenpitkin.com/depts/41/plan_historictraining.cfm) which is also very informative for anyone looking to do historic preservation work.

For leads on local preservation training and projects, go to your state office of historic preservation (www.nps.gov/history/nr/shpolist.htm lists all state Web sites as well as other preservation links). For a list of Technical Preservation Services documents on historic preservation techniques, go to www.nps.gov/history/hps/tps/ publications.htm.

Safety Training

Those of a certain age and gender—meaning younger and male—tend to believe they're indestructible; or at least that they have the ability to recover quickly from injury. This is a nice way of saying too many young men are complete knuckleheads when it comes to their own safety. If you expect to get to work every day and not have downtime due to dumb accidents, you have to address your safety and that of any employees and customers near your job site. Recommended safety measures include:

- Personal protective gear against noise, fumes, dust, and solvents
- Refusing to use damaged tools
- Allowing for fall protection when working from heights that call for it
- Wearing appropriate footwear for slippery surfaces and walking around debris
- Not creating tripping hazards
- Checking that power and water are off before working on electrical and plumbing jobs

Safety training is a major concern for big general contractors, particularly those who construct commercial buildings and large structures. On these jobs, the potential hazards increase in number and severity due to greater heights, a larger workforce, more power tools, and falling objects, including debris. These are super-sized situations compared with you, the handyman, installing a fan on a 9-foot-tall ceiling. Nevertheless, you need to keep it safe. You'll find yourself working alone at times, and you don't want to be in a situation where you're lying injured and unable to get any help.

OSHA Assistance

The U.S. Department of Labor's Occupational Safety and Health Administration (OSHA), the entity that creates workplace safety laws, has a free On-Site Consultation Service for small- to medium-sized businesses to help them identify workplace hazards and find safety solutions to them. This program is voluntary, does not impose any fines if hazards are discovered, and is administered by individual state governments. Even though a handyman's job site will change regularly, this free service could be of some benefit to you if you have any concerns over your work practices or those of your employees.

To learn more about the On-Site Consultation Service, go to www.osha.gov/dcsp/smallbusiness/consult.html, which also has links to all the appropriate state government agencies that administer the program locally.

OSHA also offers a range of publications on workplace safety and hazard prevention at their main Web site (www.osha.gov/).

If you're looking for books on safety, a search on "workplace safety books" will yield a wide range of titles.

OSHA and NIOSH

In addition to OSHA, the National Institute for Occupational Safety and Health (NIOSH) offers workplace safety publications. Go to www.cdc.gov/niosh/ and snoop around.

Law School

It always helps to have some understanding of the laws that will affect your handyman business. You're already acquainted with the various tax regulations, but you'll also be involved with contracts, liability, possible accusations of theft, and employment laws. Some law libraries have legal self-help books, as do some public libraries, but Nolo (www.nolo.com) is a prime source for legal information books and articles for small businesses and consumers. The Berkeley, California–based company has been in business since 1971, producing "easy-to-use, plain English" books and software.

13 | Business Endgame

If you follow the recommendations found in the previous chapters of this book, you will be up and running, fixing homeowners' woes from one end of town to the other. As your client base grows, along with your reputation, you'll be busier, and you'll learn how to juggle your schedule to accommodate trips to your suppliers, working the jobs, giving telephone estimates, and doing the evening bookkeeping. You'll spend some time honing your vision of the business and continually strive toward achieving it.

You will experience pitfalls, incorrect estimates, kind and thoughtful customers, nutty customers, creative solutions you hadn't considered before, some workdays that are far too long, and others that were too short and lacking in income to ever want to repeat them. In other words, this is the normal life of a small business owner.

You're Established; Now What?

The handyman business is very oriented toward a solo operation. Few handyman jobs require a second pair of hands, and you can do most of them with a small number of tools and equipment. In a normal economy, you can make a decent living for years to come working alone out of a compact car. There is always something to repair or remodel in a home, and money to be spent doing it.

Harvard University's Joint Center for Housing Studies estimates that U.S. consumers spend over $200 billion a year on home improvement and maintenance. As much as homeowners try to do their own work, there are roadblocks. A 2003 publication by Texas A&M University's Instructional Materials Service, titled "Careers in Home Maintenance and Improvement," states, "In previous generations, hand tool skills and 'know-how' were passed down from father to son. As our society has changed, this is no longer the rule. Many of today's homeowners did not learn these mechanical skills as a part of growing up." Owens Corning's 1996 "House/Work: A Study of American Homeowners" found that 90 percent of surveyed homeowners believed "home improvement and maintenance is too complicated, costly and time-consuming," while 68 percent found they could not get reliable maintenance help. This study is a bit dated, but Jerry McCarthy of Building Systems Inspection and Analysis in San Mateo, California (*Realty Times*, November 26, 2003), stated that of the 10,000 homes he had inspected during his career, over 50 percent had roofing and electrical problems and 40–50 percent had plumbing and water-related problems. A more recent 2007 American Housing Survey, a joint project of the U.S. Department of Housing and Urban Development and the U.S. Census Bureau, found that home maintenance was not priority. Of the 75,647,000 owners surveyed, 29,335,000 spent less than $25 per month on maintenance. Translation: There is a ton of maintenance work to do, whether it be deferred, preventative, or unexpected.

In a depressed economy such as the one we're experiencing now, more homeowners will attempt their own repairs or put them off, but eventually, the work will be done. You might have to adjust your rates, do some bartering, even offer to finance some larger jobs, but with some imagination, you'll stay in business.

A solo practice during challenging times will keep your cost structure down and allow for a lot of flexibility—but would you like to go further?

Time to Widen Your Vision?

Working alone means doing most tasks yourself—but there are alternatives that don't include full-time employees:

- Hiring other contractors or temporary labor as needed
- Using professionals for your accounting needs
- Having a supplier's delivery service to get materials to a job site

For some personalities, doing everything alone is both satisfying and less aggravating than working with employees; for others, it doesn't work so well after a few years. This could be due to:

- fatigue and the feeling of being stretched too thin;
- a lack of certain handyman skills that would be useful to know; or
- loneliness from lack of companionship.

> **Taxi Run**
>
> If you're in a real time crunch and need some materials to finish a job, have a taxi pick them up at your supplier and deliver them to you. This isn't a luxury if it means you'll stay on schedule instead of stopping a job to do a materials run.

Even if you like working alone, will it get you where you want to be professionally, or financially? For some people in some professions, with very specialized skills, it works out very well. Elliott Glass, for example, is *the* reviewing architect in New York City, according to a 2008 *New York Times* article. He is a master of the city's convoluted building code, bills out at $350 an hour (in 2008) to a never-ending client list, and what he says goes. As a handyman, you would need an awfully unique skill to be in a similar position, albeit at lower fees.

Small can be beautiful, but it's also limiting.

Lifestyle Choices

Working alone brings a lot of freedom. Some is illusory (if the money isn't there, how real is the freedom of having more time if you don't have freedom from want?) and some very real. You can go surfing when the waves are high, spend an afternoon at the movies, or go back to school part-time and not have to request time off from anyone.

The other side of this Huckleberry Finn journey of eternal rafting down the sunny Mississippi is taking on such a large workload that you have little time to do anything but eat, sleep, and get to the next job. If you're ambitious enough to become self-employed, you will most likely find yourself working longer hours and more days than when you were an employee somewhere else. This is an easy trap to fall into because:

- You start feeling like every job could be your last one, so you had better take it.
- Every time you tell yourself you're going to cut back, you don't, but take on more work instead.
- It's hard to give up the money.

Those Pesky Kids

How you run your business doesn't just affect you if you have a partner or a family. When you work excessive hours and then come home and fret about your workload or getting invoices out or having to wake up early the next day, all the while barely seeing those you live with, the price of running a business can shoot up dramatically. This increased price doesn't show up on any balance sheet, but you'll be more than aware of it. You have to provide what money can buy, but you also need to provide the emotional support and role modeling that comes with family life.

As your family grows or your material desires change, you'll need more income. There's only so much you can do alone. What are your alternatives?

You have several:

- Hire employees.
- Use temporary labor more often.
- Contract more work out.
- Develop high-paying specialties.

Whichever you choose, try and see it as the business evolving and your life improving.

Employees

The cost of employees has been discussed in other chapters, but there are some benefits:

- More jobs, which lead to more exposure, which leads to yet more jobs
- Increased income once employees are trained to your standards
- Potentially less hands-on work for you
- Once an employee reaches supervisor level, easier for you to take time off
- Some employees will become possible purchasers of the business should you decide to sell

Over the years, I've often had other contractors tell me to "just hire a bunch of guys" and let them do all the work. This mythical bunch of guys would, of course, show up on time, require no instruction, work efficiently, and always have a great attitude. I watched these same contractors with their guys and thought otherwise of their hiring suggestions. One painter told me, "After five guys, I might as well hire another ten; the headaches are the same." On the other hand, another painter had a superintendent who was so fast and accurate that the rest of the crew struggled to keep up with him—and as the superintendent, he wasn't expected to do that much hands-on work at all!

Employees will vary as much as any other group of human beings. Should you decide to expand in this direction, you'll need to consider:

- Recruiting
- Training
- Maintaining enough work so you're not laying people off and having to rehire later
- Your ability and willingness to manage

Managing a staff is an entirely different role than doing hands-on work. Many contractors start out small, either alone or with a partner, and gradually add a crew. One crew grows to two or three, plus an office staff, and then the company founder(s) gradually take on management roles. A good number find this a relief after years of doing the dirty work, while others miss being in the field and will occasionally go out on a job just to get out of the office.

If your game plan is to eventually grow into a larger company, figure out a time frame and guide the business in that direction.

Temporary Laborers

Agencies such as Manpower (www.manpower.com) provide a range of workers in the construction trades. Be prepared to closely supervise, as:

- Workers are trying to adapt to your standards and work practices, which can be different than their own.
- Each worker's abilities vary and are unknown to you—at least until you work together for a while.
- You would expect to supervise anyone new to you, whether a temp worker or a full-time direct employee.

Temporary laborers (temps) allow you to take on jobs you cannot safely do alone, or jobs that can be done by unskilled labor—extensive clean-up, for example—yet still be profitable for you. If you build up a relationship with a local temp agency, you could probably request a specific laborer whom you've found to be competent. By scheduling the jobs that call for additional help, you can be assured of reliable help without hiring permanent employees. For instance, you could put aside every other Monday for these jobs and, with a temp lined up, get right to work. The key will be consistently reliable temps, and it will take some time to establish this reliability with the temp agency.

Contracting Out

Hiring other contractors is a tricky area, as it can border on being a general contractor, which is an entirely different occupation than handyman and has its own requirements. The state of Minnesota, for instance, says this about residential building contractors:

> *The Department of Labor and Industry licenses residential building contractors, remodelers, roofers and manufactured home installers. The department requires certain standards of education and professional conduct be maintained to obtain and retain a license. Licenses are required for all residential building contractors and residential remodelers who contract with a homeowner to construct or improve dwellings by offering more than one special skill.*

A general contractor supervises specialty or subcontractors for a fee. As a licensed handyman, you didn't sign up for this, and your license doesn't allow for such activity. However, if you find yourself bidding a job involving multiple projects and you either cannot get to all of them, or are really getting tired of doing tile work, you can provide the customer with the name of a tile contractor who can then, under separate agreement, bid the work. Simply facilitating the direct hiring of another contractor for a customer and informally assisting with defining the job and the scheduling should fall well within your legally allowable work.

Specialty Work

In every line of work, there are specialists. A lawyer might practice family law or take on civil cases, or handle bankruptcy, divorce, corporate, or tax law. Some plumbers specialize in new construction, installing fire-suppressing sprinkler systems, fitting natural gas lines, or working with commercial steam pipes. A handyman does a variety of jobs, but you can still specialize in some which can be more lucrative than general repairs. These jobs include:

- Plaster work
- Plumbing repairs, especially emergency repairs
- Roofing leaks
- Lock repairs

Plastering was once a common trade, but no longer. True plaster repairs—not just cutting out a damaged area and replacing it with drywall—are time-consuming and require a fine touch. Repairing decorative plaster such as crown molding or ceiling medallions is even more specialized. If you live in an area with older, high-end homes, you could develop this niche and do very well by it.

Plumbers are costly and not without justification. You can't get along without a functioning plumbing system, and the work isn't exactly glamorous. As a handyman, you won't be doing major plumbing repairs, but if you're willing to come out after hours, during a holiday, or in the middle of the night to fix a sudden leak or a broken toilet in a one-bathroom house, you should be able to charge close to what a licensed plumber would charge.

A roof leak can lead to expensive ceiling repairs. Even running out and securing a tarp to the suspected source of the leak during rainy weather can be a profitable and fast job. The follow-up, the repair itself, is a second service call. Some roofers, like plumbers, offer twenty-four-hour emergency service, and their rates reflect their availability.

You probably don't want to be a full-service locksmith, but break-ins, domestic disputes, and lost keys can all result in a need for lock replacement and other security measures. If your customers know you offer this service, it could prove to be a good sideline. Bear in mind that unlike the services listed above, locksmiths need to carry more inventory and tools than a normal handyman, which can make it less appealing as something you might want to offer.

Grunt Work

Eventually, everyone finds part of their profession they just want to avoid. For a painter, it's stripping and prepping a badly peeling house. Dealing with a large volume of bird droppings—regardless of the trade—isn't anyone's idea of job fulfillment. Electricians dread dealing with unsafe live wiring done by homeowners and untrained contractors. After some time in the business, you'll run across jobs you would prefer not to do, either because of their nature or because the profit margin is too low.

When you're busy and booked up for weeks to come, you can skip these jobs or put them off until you really need work. Ideally, you want to build the business up to the point where you never have to take them, at least without charging enough to make them worth your time (and perhaps your disdain). As your business matures and you gather experience, you can eliminate certain jobs from your handyman repertoire, *providing their elimination doesn't reduce your overall business.*

For example, you might never want to climb on a roof again, but if referred customers request roof and gutter repairs and you won't do them, word gets back to the customers who originally referred you and this can affect future referrals. When you have a very solid base of work other than the jobs you want to cut out, consider making the break. Think of this as tweaking your original business plan, which was meant to serve as a guide, not an unalterable document.

Bigger, But Not Always Better, Customers

After establishing yourself with smaller businesses and residential clients, is it time to look at more-commercial accounts? Earlier marketing sections mentioned introducing yourself to property managers and real estate offices. Some maintenance companies specifically cater to apartment owners and stay quite busy, although their scope of work often includes acting as general contractors as well. Now might be the time to pursue more—or even exclusively—nonresidential work, with the following caveats:

- Commercial clients can't wait. They need the work done now, not when you can get around to it. This means you'll probably need employees.

- A few major customers will be providing most if not all of your work. This can be a disadvantage if they change handymen or tighten up on their budgets and you find yourself with less work to do and no residential work to fall back on.
- Payments can be slower.
- Big property managers have numerous apartments and offices under their control, and there's often work to do somewhere.

In cities with rent control, there is apparently less apartment turnover in controlled units and, depending on who's commenting, more deferred maintenance which can't be deferred forever. In standard markets, turnover means a certain percentage of units will need to be cleaned, painted, and updated aside from normal maintenance. Either way, if you can stick to your pricing and establish good working relationships with property managers, this could be a new and preferred direction for your business.

There Are More Homes Than Businesses

Even if you go in the direction of commercial clients, it isn't a bad idea to maintain some residential work as filler if nothing else. Also, given the downturn in the current economy, the more options for work you have, the better.

Time to Close Up Shop

Some people stay in the same profession or run their businesses for years and years, eventually retiring. Others can't take whatever they're doing for more than a few years and move on to another job or an entirely different line of work (such as starting a handyman business). For the most part, when we have obligations—usually this means a family—we stick with what we're doing if the money is steady and there's some degree of contentment with the work itself. You'll know it's time to get out of the business when you:

- never want to fix anything again;
- have too many dreams—or nightmares—about home repairs;

- feel like the business is more a burden than a benefit;
- find the financial returns aren't worth the work and the fretting;
- have enough money or the promise of a new career that you can afford to leave; or when you
- realize the thrill is gone.

Some business owners plan from the beginning to sell out after a certain time period has passed, or a certain income level is reached. Others sell due to age, illness, a change of personal circumstances, or simply the desire to do something different. Whatever your reasons, you should be prepared for the sale.

What You're Selling

When you sell your business, you're selling the company's:

- assets (tools, office equipment, vehicles);
- reputation; and
- client list and contracts.

A sole proprietorship with one truck and a small number of tools (most of which you'll probably keep) is selling a reputation and its clients. The same is true when a physician or dentist sells a practice: The purchaser is really buying the patients, who presumably will stay with the new owner of the practice. You will have more to sell if you have maintenance contracts with property managers or business owners. There is less to sell when you have some repeat residential customers but mostly depend on new clients for your livelihood. You are then selling an established name, but really no guarantees of future business.

A larger concern with, say, thirty employees, a dozen trucks, a garage full of equipment and materials, and its own small office building has more tangible assets. Whatever size business you're selling, a price will need to be determined and agreed upon.

Pre-Sale

Once you've decided to sell the business and you've established a timeline, you will need to "pretty it up" for a potential buyer. The first thing to do is assess the business finances and procedures.

- Be sure all transactions are current and recorded.
- Prepare audited financial statements with graph presentations of revenue growth.

- If you have any special arrangements with certain customers or employees, either formalize them in writing or eliminate them.
- Write a summary of all your supplier information and discounts.
- Update all company procedures and policies in clear, written manual form.
- Describe, in writing, any office or equipment leases.
- List all the company assets that go along with the sale.

If your books are in order, your financial statements should be relatively easy to prepare. The remaining information, even if you don't sell the company according to your time frame, is good to have on hand for your own sake.

Setting a Price

What's your company worth? It's worth whatever you can get for it, of course. As the owner, though, how objective will you be? You've built a successful business from scratch, and you've worked a lot of late hours to do it. That all counts for something, but determining the value of all your efforts is somewhat emotional, whereas looking at the numbers is more objective.

Some ways of determining the value of your business include:

- Comparing your business with similar handyman businesses bought and sold in your area
- Earnings capitalization
- An agreed-upon multiple of yearly revenue

It will be pretty tough figuring out what other handyman businesses sell for given there's no huge market or clearinghouse for them. You can't really compare it to a franchised handyman business, as that's a different animal altogether. A good CPA with small-business experience would be helpful, both to compare yours with like businesses and to do an accurate review of your books.

Earnings capitalization means the purchaser figures a desired rate of return on the amount of money spent purchasing the business. The earnings determine the return. If the business has traditionally earned $60,000 and the purchaser wants at least a 20 percent return, then the purchase price could be as high as $300,000. It's an imperfect calculation, of course, since the earnings can always change, but the longer you've maintained a certain earnings level, the better.

You and a buyer might agree to a multiple of the company's revenue as a purchase price. A business with $90,000 in revenue, if purchased at two times revenue, would sell for $180,000. However, revenue is one thing, and earnings—what you have left over after you figure out the cost of doing business—is something else (a much smaller something else). Revenue could be $180,000, but earnings only $70,000. Smarter buyers would look at earnings.

There are intangibles to consider, such as goodwill, which is difficult to quantify. If you're a sole proprietor and you've created all this goodwill and a solid reputation, then *you* are essentially the company. Once you're gone, doesn't that all go with you, waiting to be reestablished by the new owner? Goodwill is worth something, but determining a value for it can be a bit elusive.

If Your Price Isn't Met . . .

You can have a realistic price for your business or a fantasy price, based not on numbers but on what you want because you want it. If you get the latter, good for you; take the money and run. When a realistic price is considered too high, then you have to decide how badly you want out and how much of a lower price you're willing to take. Try to avoid desperately needing to sell the business, either for personal or financial reasons. (I know—far easier said than done if you are indeed in desperate circumstances.)

Do you need to adjust your time frame? Currently, credit is tight and potential buyers without ready cash might have trouble borrowing enough to buy you out. You're not completely stuck when the economy is down, though, as you can still consider:

- Financing the sale yourself by selling on a contract
- Putting off the sale for six to twelve months, or until a buyer appears
- Taking on a partner and gradually backing yourself out of the business

No solution is perfect, but you cannot control economic realities, only adapt to them.

Letting Go

Once you've sold the company, you have no control over how it's run or its future. You might find the new owner's direction or level of service appalling, or very impressive. Either way, despite any emotional attachment that still lingers, all you can do is watch and perhaps offer some occasional advice if you know the new owner well enough to do so.

Otherwise, let it go. Start up a new company if you want, but let this one go. You've done your job, and presumably did it well, and it's time to move on to something else. If you did well by the business, be glad for that, and for what you learned from it.

But Should You Sell?

Some sellers regret their decisions and buy their businesses back. Charles Schwab, of the brokerage firm Charles Schwab & Company, purchased his company back from Bank of America six years after selling it to them. He then took the company public and became very wealthy in the process.

Appendix A
Hiring and Firing Employees

As soon as you start hiring employees, you're subject to federal and state laws which spell out what hiring practices you must abide by. These practices range from safety standards to illegal discrimination. They are basically overwritten legalese versions of everything you should have learned in kindergarten, including play fair, show some concern for others, don't create unnecessarily dangerous situations, and being a jerk isn't in your best interest.

Some laws kick in when you have a certain number of employees, usually fifteen or more, but state laws might have different criteria and affect smaller employers. The federal laws that affect all employers include:

- The Employee Polygraph Protection Act (EPPA)
- The Fair Labor Standards Act (FLSA)
- The Occupational Safety and Health (OSH) Act
- Uniformed Services Employment and Reemployment Rights Act (USERRA)
- Whistle-Blower Protections
- The Immigration Control And Reform Act (IRCA—right to work in the USA)

Swell, you say; what do all these mean?

- Polygraph protection means, essentially, that you can't mandate an employee take a polygraph test; there are exceptions for some jobs in the security business, or in the case of suspected employee theft.
- The FLSA covers wages, including overtime and minimum wages ($7.25 an hour for 2009) and related issues (go to www.dol.gov/esa/whd/regs/compliance/whd_fs.pdf for a wage and hour information sheet).

- The Occupational Safety and Health Act regulates, on a federal level, safe working conditions. Each state has its own safety requirements which can exceed those of OSHA.
- USERRA protects reemployment rights for those returning from a period of deployment in the uniformed services, including those called up from the reserves or National Guard, and prohibits employer discrimination based on military service or obligation.
- Whistle-blower Protections prohibit recrimination against any employee who turns you in for unsafe or unfair work practices.
- IRCA requires employers to document, within three working days, an employee's eligibility and right to work in the USA. The U.S. Department of Homeland Security has an I-9 form (effective until 6/30/09) that all employees must submit. It verifies two facts about an employee: 1) the right to work in the US and 2) personal identity. A new I-9 form will be available after 6/30/09. (Go to www.uscis.gov/files/form/I-9.pdf). You must keep these forms on file for three years after the date of hire and one year after employee termination.

Your state's Department of Labor and Industries will have information on applicable state laws for fair employment and workplace practices.

You Can Be Discriminating, but You Can't Discriminate

If the world is looked at objectively, there's no such thing as race—just humans who, over thousands of years, adapted to different climates. The results? Different sizes, skin colors, and body features, all of which we have managed to attribute highly undeserved degrees of social importance. Thus, we classify ourselves by race, among other categories.

As an employer, you can't discriminate by race in your hiring practices. You can, and should, hire the best people you can find and leave it at that. You can make these determinations by:

- Gathering background and past job information
- Administering a written test (e.g., how to estimate the amount of paint needed for an exterior, the correct way to ensure a fence is level or following a slope properly, etc.)
- Discussing the company's pricing and work policies to be sure the candidate for the job agrees with them

■ Having the candidate take you through a simple job, such as installing a door, so you can ascertain a competency level

When it comes to age, you can't hire someone too young (www.youthrules.dol.gov/states.htm for state minimum age laws), and, if you have more than twenty employees, you can't, for the most part, discriminate against anyone forty years of age or older.

For All to See

Federal and state laws require you to display official labor and employment posters detailing applicable labor laws. They must be posted where employees can easily read them. These are available free of charge from your state office of Labor and Industries and from the Department of Labor (www.dol.gov/osbp/welcome.htm). For more small-business information from the Department of Labor, go to www.dol.gov/osbp/sbrefa/main.htm.

Once you've hired an employee, you should follow up with appropriate training both for the customer's sake and your own, as you don't want to send someone to a job site with insufficient ability to do the job properly. Training should include:

■ How to dress for the job (company uniform or acceptable clothing)
■ Comportment on the job site
■ Familiarity with the products used on each job, along with their proper handling and installation
■ Scheduling and time management
■ Billing and collecting payments due
■ Any and all administrative work done in the field
■ Promoting the company
■ Noting any additional work the customer might need and offering an estimate for it

Firing Practices

Throughout the United States, work "at-will" is the law of the land. The Employment at Will doctrine means that employment is voluntary for both employees and employers. With the exception of Montana, "at-will" allows a nongovernment employer to terminate employees who are not under contract for a specified period of time for any legal reason, or without any reason at all, at any time. It also allows an employee to leave or resign just as abruptly. This does not mean you're free to assume the crown of royalty and dismiss your employees like so many tenant farming peasants you'd like to force off the land. Arbitrary dismissal can lead to expensive discrimination claims if the dismissal is found to be wrongful or discriminatory. Various court cases have resulted in a state-by-state interpretation of the at-will relationship, so it's imperative that you understand the laws in the state in which you will be doing business.

Overall, you cannot fire an employee for:

- Discrimination based on race, color, religion, sex, age, disability, or national origin
- Filing workers' compensation claims
- Union membership
- Fulfilling jury service
- Being called up for military service
- Refusing to perform an illegal act, or, in some cases, reporting an illegal act ("whistle-blowing")

If you live in Montana, you need to be aware of the Wrongful Discharge from Employment Act, which calls for "reasonable, job-related grounds for dismissal based on a failure to perform job duties satisfactorily, disruption of the employer's operation or other legitimate business reason."

Sounds a bit ominous, doesn't it? You want to control whom you hire and let go without worrying about meeting jury duty requirements or the specifics of civil rights legislation. You can, but you'll need to establish some processes and procedures to stay legal, protect your business, and do the right thing for your employees. To prevent the wrongful discharge of an employee, consider the following:

- Know your specific state laws and local laws in regard to termination; your department of Labor and Industries can supply these and offer counsel if you have any questions. In many states you must allow employees time off to vote in elections; in twenty states, employees are paid while taking the time to vote. Other states have specific pregnancy laws that differ from the Family and Medical Leave Act, including the size of the company that's affected (far fewer than the minimum fifty employees as stated in the Family and Medical Leave Act). Inquire with your state employment office for specific laws that apply to you.

- During the hiring interview, fully explain the nature of the work expected of the employee and document this explanation, having the prospective employee sign off as understanding the demands of the job. This way, someone cannot come back later and claim, for instance, that working conditions would be dusty or a certain amount of weight would have to be lifted and moved about.

- Establish written company employment policies in an employee handbook, outlining everything from the number and length of breaks, including lunch during a full working day to time off for jury duty to attendance at mandatory meetings for which the employee will be paid, to weather-related and emergency closures. Explain the concept of "at-will" work and the reasons for termination. Be sure every employee gets a copy of these policies and review them from time to time during your company meetings. Note in the handbook that policies can change without prior notice, but the changes will be published and distributed. Have each employee sign off as having read and understood the handbook, and keep a copy of this in each employee's personnel file.

- Establish a grievance procedure stating how an employee can report violations to the company policies or laws, be it an anonymous or recognized reporting. Include an appeal process should an employee not agree with a management decision that affects that employee.

- Establish and publish a disciplinary process for employees whose work or conduct is not up to company expectations. The process should include oral and written warnings, progressive discipline—such as suspension or administrative leave during an investigation—fair application of the process, an opportunity for the employee to respond, and full documentation and recordkeeping of each disciplinary action.

Regardless of the applicability of any specific law, a dismissed employee can try and bring legal proceedings against you for wrongful termination. This can be time-consuming and expensive for you, so it's imperative you understand the laws, provide clear oral and written communication to your employees, and keep careful logs and records (a paper trail) of any disciplinary actions. The more open your communications with your employees, the less likely any will seek redress against you for real or imagined issues.

As long as you aren't violating the law, you can dismiss an employee, even if your reasoning seems arbitrary. You simply have to be sure your reasoning can't be shown to look too much like a violation of a legal protection. One exception to this type of dismissal is if you and your employee signed a contract that covered a specific period of time. In that case, you can't terminate without good cause unless the contract has a clause stating either party can end the agreement without any consequence.

Your employees have some responsibilities, too. They must take all required breaks during the work day at the normal times; they cannot bank these times and leave early or come in late. Some exceptions can be made when the nature of the work prevents taking a break. For instance, the weather takes a severe turn and you have to get some doors installed before a storm starts. Check with your state's Department of Labor and Industries for specific guidelines.

In some parts of the country, and depending on the amount and types of commercial work you do, you might be faced with unionizing your company should your employees vote union. For better or for worse, union ranks have shrunk considerably in the last fifty years, from 35 percent of the wage and salary workforce to approximately 12.4 percent in 2008, according to the Bureau of Labor Statistics. With some industry-specific exceptions, Right to Work laws in over twenty states allow employees to choose whether or not to join or financially support a union at their place of work, although they can benefit from a union-negotiated contract. The following states have Right to Work laws:

Alabama, Arizona, Arkansas, Florida, Georgia, Idaho, Indiana (school employees only), Iowa, Kansas, Louisiana, Mississippi, Nebraska, Nevada, North Carolina, North Dakota, Oklahoma, South Carolina, South Dakota, Tennessee, Texas, Utah, Virginia, and Wyoming

Holidays

You don't *have* to stop working on any holidays, but you'll find yourself working alone if you don't recognize at least some of the following ten national holidays:

- New Year's Day
- Martin Luther King Junior's Birthday
- Washington's Birthday or Presidents Day
- Memorial Day
- Independence Day
- Labor Day
- Columbus Day
- Veterans Day
- Thanksgiving Day
- Christmas Day

You only have to pay your regular hourly rate for holiday work unless working a holiday exceeds a forty-hour week. You don't have to give paid holiday leave, either, should you choose to close down for any given holiday. Many companies traditionally offer some paid holidays, however. You don't have to offer paid vacations, either, although if you want to remain competitive and attract good employees, you'll most likely offer some kind of package that includes holidays off, some with pay, and paid vacation days. These benefits are strictly a matter of negotiation between you and your employees. The law doesn't force you to provide paid holidays, days off, vacations, or sick days. But good business sense will take you in this direction.

Appendix B
How to Figure Your Costs

You have to know your costs, or a close approximation, in order to know what to charge so you can walk away with a profit. When you're working alone, this accounting is simpler. Whether it's just you or you and an employee (or more than one), it's easy to discount or exclude some of the time you spend on the business; for instance, the evenings you spend going over the books, or the weekend estimates. You probably won't bill for every minute of your time, but you should include as much as possible into your overhead estimates. Overhead includes:

- License, bond, and all insurance coverage (vehicle, business, disability, and medical)
- Office expenses
- Equipment purchases and maintenance
- Accounting and legal help
- Marketing
- Your time spent with customers and billings
- Business and occupation taxes

Overhead can vary from a shoestring budget to one that would cover an on-call London boot maker. For that reason, coming up with a hard-and-fast figure for the sake of an example is a thankless exercise. However, let's assume $400 a month for overhead for a sole proprietor just getting started, keeping in mind it covers previously personal expenses such as vehicle insurance and cell-phone coverage, as these are now, at least in part, business expenses. You can always adjust the figures to match your circumstances. Then there's the cost of employees.

There are a number of ways to account for the cost of an employee, meaning some costs are included as overhead and some as labor. All include:

- Hourly rates paid
- Social Security and Medicare contributions
- FUTA (Federal Unemployment Taxes) and SUTA (State Unemployment Taxes)*
- State Disability
- Paid vacation, sick, and personal days
- Allowance for vehicles or mileage
- Retirement programs

Hourly pay varies all over the country. For the sake of this example, assume fifteen dollars an hour per employee.

- Basic hourly wage $15.00
- Social Security and Medicare @ 7.65 percent = $1.15
- Workers' Compensation @ 6.6 percent or $1.00 (varies with each state; 6.6 percent assumed for this example)
- Hourly subtotal = $17.15
- $450 for FUTA and SUTA* or 22.5 cents an hour
- 68 cents an hour for paid time off**
- Hourly subtotal = $18.08
- $2.40 for overhead***
- Hourly total = $20.48

Some advise simply adding a fixed percentage—30 or 40 percent, or even 100 percent—to an employee's hourly rate to cover all costs, but that's not very exacting. The above example is very basic, and can be tailored to meet your circumstances and costs, which will vary. If you're working alone, for instance, your base hourly rate will be higher, and your Social Security and Medicare will double, but you will not be paying FUTA or SUTA.

*FUTA (Federal Unemployment Taxes): 6.2 percent for the first $7,000 of salary, but a 5.4 percent credit is applied for SUTA (State Unemployment Taxes) you pay

**Ten paid holidays, sick days, and personal days: eighty hours at $17.15 hour equals $1,372, or .68 an hour ($1,372 divided into 2,000 working hours. There are a possible 2,080 yearly working hours based on a forty-hour week; eighty hours are removed for paid holidays, etc.)

***$4,800 a year, or 2,000 working hours. However, you, the owner, are also covered by this overhead, so the $2.40 figure can be reduced to a fraction of that applied per employee.

The $20.48 an hour is your cost per employee, but you're free to bill out at whatever rate you wish. Some will add on for profit only (see below), and others will charge a percentage of their own rate as the business owner, similar to the difference between a journeyman rate and that of an apprentice. If you charge too little, the whole business will get old quickly, and if you charge too much, you won't have enough business. Look at the industry standards for your area and bill accordingly.

What to Charge

For one discussion on what to charge, go to www.woodweb.com/knowledge_base/Overhead_per_employee.html.

There are two more factors to consider when establishing your costs: materials and profit.

Materials

Although you should figure the cost of your time when ordering and picking up materials, you have to decide whether you're going to mark them up or not. Some contractors point out in their advertising that they have no markups, and they provide copies of their receipts with their billings. Others simply add on 10 percent at a minimum. This is strictly a personal decision, as there is no right or wrong direction to go.

Profit

When a contractor ends up "working for wages," it means the job was underbid and the only money earned is an hourly wage. You want to cover all your costs, including your established hourly rate, but you want a profit on top of this. Why? Because you're taking a lot of risks running your own business, and your profit is the reward for those risks. When everything is going gangbusters, some might think your profit on top of your other fees is excessive, but you'll hear few empathetic comments from those same people when you haven't had any work for weeks on end because of a crashed economy or your inability to work due to an accident.

A 10 percent profit added on to the cost of a bill isn't out of line. Some contractors, at least on large jobs, negotiate their profit and add it on as a line item on their billings. For a handyman business, it's best to include it in your rates, including that of your employees. Adding 10 percent to our hypothetical $20.48/hour employee brings the hourly rate to $22.53/hour. Many contractors simply bill out at double the rate they pay their workers. This is a safe strategy that should cover costs and unexpected circumstances while yielding a decent profit.

Resources

Web Sites

Business
Small Business Administration, www.sba.gov
Business Plans and Financing:

> www.sba.gov/smallbusinessplanner/plan/writeabusinessplan/index.html

> www.sba.gov/services/financialassistance/index.html (financial programs)

> http://usgovinfo.about.com/od/smallbusiness/a/stategrants.htm (state small business programs)

> www.ethnicmajority.com/Government_MBE_programs.htm (minority programs)

> www.mbda.gov (Minority Business Development Agency)

> www.business.gov/start/woman-owned (women-owned business programs)

> Service Corps of Retired Executives (SCORE), www.score.org/index.html

> Microsoft Business Start-up (http://office.microsoft.com/en-us/help/HA011602011033.aspx)

Wage and Pay Scale Comparisons:

> U.S. Department of Labor (www.dol.gov)

> PayScale (www.payscale.com)

> www.costhelper.com (costs for various home repair jobs)

Intuit QuickBase Consultant:

> Cullen Coates, cwcoates@cullencoates.com

Human Resources Consultant for Small Businesses:

> Dark Horse Consulting, Jeanette Monahan, jmmonahan44@yahoo.com

Insurance

www.ehealthinsurance.com (costs and policy availability figures)

www.entrepreneur.com/insurancecenter (primer on business insurance)

National Association of Insurance Commissioners, www.naic.org (research potential insurance carriers)

Licensing

www.sba.gov/hotlist/license.html (list of state licensing bureaus)

www.businesslicenses.com/ and www.businessnameusa.com (fee-based companies that assist in business licensing)

Bond

Surety & Fidelity Association of America, www.surety.org (information on surety companies)

Legal

www.nolo.com (do-it-yourself, easy-to-use law books and software)

www.lawyers.com (to check out prospective lawyers)

Software

Accounting

Intuit's QuickBooks (http://quickbooks.intuit.com/)

Microsoft Small Office Accounting (www.microsoft.com/smallbusiness/products/Financial-Management.aspx)

Peachtree Complete Accounting Software (www.peachtree.com/peachtree accountingline/)

Office

Google Docs, http://docs.google.com/templates (freeware, online storage, and multiple-user access)

NeoOffice, www.neooffice.org (freeware word processing for Apple platform)

Microsoft Office Suite (www.microsoft.com)

Adobe Acrobat (www.adobe.com)

Intuit QuickBase (http://quickbase.intuit.com/)

Taxes

TurboTax (www.turbotax.com)

Tax Act series from Second Story Software (www.taxact.com)

Web Site Construction

Microsoft Expression Web 2 (www.microsoft.com/expression/products/purchase .aspx?key=Web)

Adobe Dreamweaver CS4 (www.adobe.com/products/dreamweaver/)

Creating and Maintaining Your Web Site

Hosting:

       Bluehost (www.bluehost.com)

       Yahoo (www.yahoo.com)

       Squidoo (free, single page only, www.squidoo.com)

       GeoCities (free, limited space, http://geocities.yahoo.com/).

Web Directory Submittal:

       www.dmoz.org

Ad Placement:

       Google AdWords (www.adwords.com)

       Craigslist (www.craigslist.com)

       Credit Card Payment Centers

       ProPay (www.propay.com)

       Pay Pal (www.paypal.com)

Social Networking:

       www.MySpace.com

       www.Facebook.com

       www.LinkedIn.com

       www.Classmates.com

       www.Twitter.com

Business Reviews:

       www.Yelp.com

Tax Information

Internal Revenue Service (www.irs.gov)

State Departments of Revenue (www.irs.gov/taxpros/article/0,,id=100236,00.html)

Marketing

Bulk Mailing Rates/Permit (http://pe.usps.com/businessmail101/welcome.htm)

iStockphoto (www.istockphoto.com)

Cole Information Services (www.coleinformation.com)

Historic Preservation Societies (www.preservationdirectory.com/Preservation OrganizationsResources/OrganizationCategories.aspx)

Product Installation Certifications

Flooring (www.nwfacp.org)

American Window and Door Institute Certified Installer (www.awdi.com/prog.html)

North American Laminate Flooring Association (www.nalfa.org/retailersInstaller CertificationClass.php)

Certified Floorcovering Installers (www.cfiinstallers.com)

Ceramic Tile Education Foundation (www.tileschool.org/)

Armstrong Certified Installer (www.floorexpert.com)

Institute of Inspection, Cleaning, and Restoration (www.iicrc.org/home.shtml)

Mr. Grab Bar (www.mrgrabbar.com)

Product/Industry Web Sites

Paint (www.sherwinwilliams.com)

National Paint and Coatings Association (www.paint.org)

Caulk and Sealants (www.dap.com)

Personal Safety Equipment (www.3m.com)

Tools and Hardware:

      Black & Decker (www.blackanddecker.com)

      Stanley (www.stanleytools.com)

      Ace Hardware (www.acehardware.com)

      Japanese Saws (www.japanwoodworker.com)

      Makita (www.makita.com)

      Lee Valley Tools (www.leevalley.com)

      Electrical (www.leviton.com)

      Flooring (www.floorexpert.com)

Safety

On the Job:

OSHA (www.osha.gov)

NIOSH (www.cdc.gov/NIOSH)

Lead-Based Paint Issues:

www.epa.gov/lead

Home Repair

Natural Handyman (www.naturalhandyman.com)

Hometime (www.hometime.com)

Do-It-Yourself (www.doityourself.com)

Home Depot (www.homedepot.com)

Lowe's (www.lowes.com)

Publications

Reader's Digest Compete Do-It-Yourself Manual

Black & Decker Books

Sunset Home Repair Books

Working Windows: A Guide to the Repair and Restoration of Wood Windows

Family Handyman

This Old House

Fine Homebuilding

Popular Mechanics

Builders Booksource (www.buildersbooksource.com)

Technical Preservation Services (www.nps.gov/history/hps/tps/publications.htm)

Temporary Contract Labor

Manpower (www.manpower.com)

Index

found items, 144
401(k), individual, 123, 124, 126
franchise opportunities, 5
freebies, 70, 169–71
furniture, 94–95, 165
FUTA (Federal Unemployment Taxes), 71, 214

G
general contractors, 63, 111, 198
general liability insurance, 61–62
Glass, Elliott, 195
golden rules, handyman's, 152
goodwill, 204
Google AdWords, 178, 182
Google Docs, 88, 103
government regulations, 12
graphic artists, 89
graphics software, 88
gravesite maintenance, 165–66
grievance procedures, 210
grunt work, 200

H
hiring employees, 206–8
historical preservation, 163–64, 190
holidays, 212
Home Depot, 167, 187
home equity lines of credit, 116
home inspectors, 162
home office deduction, 134, 135
home-repair guides, 171, 188–89
home shows, 169–70, 172
home warranty companies, 163
home work space, 94–106
hourly fees, 72–73, 146

I
I-9 form, 141, 207
Immigration Control and Reform Act (IRCA), 206, 207
income, 71–75, 127, 128, 143–44, 145
independent contractors, 29–30
Individual Retirement Accounts (IRAs), 122–24, 125–26
insurance
    automobile, 59, 61, 63
    business, 12, 19–21, 62
    disability, 58, 59–60
general liability, 61–62
importance of, 63, 78
medical, 58, 60–61
paying for, 78, 114
shopping for, 58–59, 77
umbrella policy, 62
insurance companies, marketing to, 161
integrity, 6
Internal Revenue Service (IRS), 29, 30, 76, 81–82, 132–33
Internet and e-commerce, 168, 175–83
introverts, 8, 11, 173
invoices, 83

J
job size, 23–24
Johnson and Johnson, 140

K
Keogh plans, 123, 126
keywords, Web site, 177

L
labels, self-adhesive foil, 91
lawyers, 65, 67, 68, 137
lead abatement, 150–51
legal and ethical issues, 139–52
liability insurance, 61–62
licenses, 12, 64, 65, 78, 79, 140–41
lifestyle choices, 195–96
lighting, 96
limited liability companies (LLC), 51–52, 132–33
LinkedIn, 154–55
lists, 11, 26–27, 49–50
locksmithing, 199–200
Lowe's, 187

M
magazines, 157, 189–90
maintenance contracts, 51
marketing, 153–74
    business plans and, 45–48
    financial planning, 69–70
    getting started, 88–91
    initial costs of, 21
materials, 67–69, 105, 149, 215
mechanic's liens, 111–12

About the Author

Terry Meany has been a contractor, landlord, columnist, and author of home repair books. He maintains a love/hate relationship with his tools and home, but keeps maintenance in check. After far too many years living in the drizzly Northwest, he and his wife are planning a move to sunnier climes. Their next home will be all concrete and built to penal institution standards, where nothing ever breaks under normal use.